To Ellen.
Best Wishes

Don Clawson
April 2009

Fig.1   Pre-aviation Cadet Clawson - 1944

IS THAT SOMETHING THE CREW SHOULD KNOW?

Irreverent Anecdotes of an Air Force Pilot

Don Clawson

ATHENA PRESS
LONDON

IS THAT SOMETHING THE CREW SHOULD KNOW?
Irreverent Anecdotes of an Air Force Pilot
Copyright © Don Clawson 2003

ISBN 1 932077 80 4

First Published 2003 by
ATHENA PRESS
Queen's House, 2 Holly Road
Twickenham TW1 4EG
United Kingdom

Printed for Athena Press

IS THAT SOMETHING THE CREW SHOULD KNOW?

Irreverent Anecdotes of an Air Force Pilot

Statement of Purpose

The purpose of writing this book is to describe some of the actual events occurring in the life of an Air Force pilot while instructing undergraduate pilot trainees in the B-25 aircraft, performing the duties of an aircraft commander in B-47 and B-52 Bombers with thermonuclear weapons involved, and finally—after 24 years of service—getting shot at on every mission while flying 122 EC-121 reconnaissance flights over all parts of Indo-China. The title is derived from an actual event, in that if the question had not been asked, we would have destroyed a valuable air force asset in the Gulf of Mexico with 750-pound iron bombs.

The book also describes the B-52 Airborne Alert mission during the Cuban Missile Crisis, called Chrome Dome. The number of Aircraft involved was not disclosed to the National Command Authority (NCA), nor was the control procedures used to assure the NCA that no one would start WWIII without permission. This was hollow and depended entirely on the integrity of the three B-52 primary crew-members. The NCA believed that there were up to 66 armed B-52s in the air at any one time, when there were more likely to be up to 176 aircraft with 616 thermonuclear weapons in the air. Reporting was done in the clear so that Soviet "listeners" could count them. Contrary to what is shown in movies like *Thirteen Days*, the weapons were not inhibited in any way and the crew had complete capability to arm and drop the weapons at any time. The EC-121 Joint chiefs of Staff controlled missions are described. These were College Eye and Igloo White. The Chiefs tried every way to deter Robert McNamara from taking the old Worn-out Navy EC-121 aircraft out of the Arizona boneyard and flying the "Electronic Fence". The concept was wrong for the time and place it was utilized, and was an utter and dismal failure in spite of the tremendous effort of thousands of people and the expenditure of and enormous amount of money.

Veterans Day

At 11:00 a.m., on this day in 1918, the fighting of World War I stopped. At first this day honored the men and women of World War I and people observed a moment of silence at the 11th hour of the 11th day of the 11th month.

Today we use the day as a time to honor the veterans of all the wars of our country. There may be a parade with marching bands, Veterans' organizations, boy and girl scouts, and other groups. The parade may end in front of a statue where a wreath is placed and speeches are made.

Do you know someone who is a veteran? Write him or her a letter of thanks for serving in our armed forces and working to protect our country. Include reasons why serving in the armed forces was an important thing to do.

Dear Veteran,

Today is Veterans Day. I want to thank you for flying in the airforce over Holland to stop Adof in worlb1 +thank you grandpa D.. I bett that B52-bomber was hard to fly wasit? Next time you visit my house can you tell me a war story about when you got shotat in the plane please? I'm glad someone served oar country. Was it scary when you were in a big war? From your, Daughter's Son, Nikolaas

lots of love, Nikolaas

Fig.2   Nikolaas's Veterans Day letter

Prolog

The motivation for recording these anecdotes and relating my experiences came from my then nine-year old grandson, Nikolaas. One day around Veterans Day he wrote me a nice note for having visited his school to give a short talk about servicemen and he asked me to come to his house and tell him a war story. Well, Nikolaas, here it is.

The day Pearl Harbor was attacked I was working in a gasoline service station. When we heard the news, the first question was "where is Pearl Harbor?" In the next few weeks and months many scary stories were related and one night it was claimed that Japanese airplanes had attempted to bomb San Pedro Harbor and many rounds of anti-aircraft ammunition were fired. One California State Guardsman even suffered a heart attack. We had blackouts and reduced lighting on automobiles and overeager Air Raid Wardens rushing about. There were small probes by Japanese submarines, but we were still concerned since most of our defenses had been lost at Pearl Harbor.

I was in high school at the time and from then on all the young men had only one outlook and that was service in one of the armed forces. Some left school early and enlisted, some under-aged and some accelerated graduation. I was given some credits for auto shop for working in the service station. I had already advanced two grades in one year when in grade school, so I graduated a month after my seventeenth birthday.

Ever since I was very small I had been attracted to flying. One of our neighbors, Lieutenant Colonel Titus, a Medal of Honor winner from the Boxer Rebellion had a son in the Army Air Corps. He used to fly over his father's house so low he took out many walnut tree limbs getting his fathers attention. He would then fly to Burbank or Glendale Airports and his father would pick him up. I could see the Captain's face as he dove at the trees. This impressed me.

We found out that we could enlist for aircrew training in the Army Air Forces when we were seventeen. We had to wait until we were eighteen before being called to active duty, so I went to

Parks Air College in Cahokia, Illinois to better prepare for pilots' school. I spent two semesters at Parks, returned to North Hollywood to await call up, and went on active duty July 1, 1944.

After fifteen months of active duty, during which nothing was accomplished as far as flying was concerned, I was discharged. February 1, 1946 I was married and returned to Parks and finished school September, 1947. In April 1947 our first daughter was born. Since I had decided to get married my father believed I could fend for myself, we almost survived on the ninety dollars a month from the VA.

After working for Pacific Bell Telephone Company for eight days I quit to find work with the U.S. Weather Bureau in Flagstaff, Arizona. Neither of these jobs paid enough to survive. The telephone company pay was $13 per week. They relied on veterans having the G.I. Bill to supplement their wages, but I had exhausted my entitlement. While in Flagstaff I requested a direct commission in the Air Force Reserve. The request went through channels and was about to be rejected when the school secretary, a Captain Long at Williams Air Force Base near Phoenix, Arizona, turned the paper over, and a secondary provision qualified me to apply. I was required to take the Officers' Qualification Test and appear before a board of officers. I received my commission in the reserve in 1948.

While many people recall serving in the Army Air Corps, in fact the Army Air Corps ceased to exist on June 30, 1941, becoming the Army Air Forces, to more accurately reflect the intended size of the build-up, and to allow promotion of General 'Hap' Arnold to five stars. I have noticed in my old records from WWII that the words 'Air Corps' lingered on in the records.

Fig.3   The coveted VD flag

7 May 1945

OFFICE OF THE COMMANDING GENERAL

SUBJECT: Diversion of Pre-Aviation Cadets

TO: Pvt Lyle D Clawson, Squadron "B".

1. The magnificent successes of our Armed Forces in the European Theater of Operations is a source of profound gratification to all of us. The world knows that one of the greatest contributing factors in the destruction of Nazi military forces has been the aggressive and heroic warfare waged by our Army Air Forces. Their part in winning the Battle of Europe is now a glowing chapter in the history of our country.

2. This victory, the date of which could not be accurately predicted, requires a new appraisal of our military needs. It will be necessary to redeploy vast amounts of materiel and large numbers of men from the European Theater to the Asiatic and Pacific combat zones. This in turn, has a direct effect on the training program of the Army Air Forces, and on you men who have been selected for aircrew training. At the present time, there are sufficient numbers of pilots, bombardiers, and navigators in the United States and among those units scheduled for redeployment to supply most of the necessary requirements. The remainder of necessary aircrew replacements will be drawn from present pre-flight, primary, basic, and advanced trainees who will complete their training in the next several months. It is deeply regretted but inevitable, therefore, that you must be withdrawn from the aircrew training program and be diverted to other assignments where you may contribute in the maximum degree to the defeat of Japan. You must consider these measures in a practical manner. We all agree that it is fortunate this favorable turn of events has made this retrenchment program possible. Army Air Forces Training plans have always made certain that we have enough trained personnel in all categories. The fact that we are ahead in our requirements has had a great deal to do with hastening the conclusion of this war.

3. On the other hand, I shall not attempt to minimize the keen disappointment I know you will suffer at being withdrawn from aircrew training through no fault of your own. I fully realize that you have been selected, tested, and qualified under very rigorous standards for this training, and that your hearts were set upon completing your training. The fact that you entered the aircrew program is proof in itself of your spirited motivation to fly and fight for your country in the air.

Fig.4   'Dear John' letter

4. You will soon be released from your status as pre-aircrew trainees without the loss of any grade you may now hold. If your present skill offers reasonable assurance of your effective utilization without further training, you may be immediately assigned to permanent party, or you may be assigned to the continental Air Forces with the possible opportunity for overseas duty. Many of you will have the privilege of entering technical training where military requirements dictate such training be given. Each of you must fully realize that you are eligible for overseas duty regardless of whether or not you are accepted for immediate duty assignment, or whether you are entered into technical training. In the event future developments require expansion of the aircrew training program, or if opportunities develop for a post-war aircrew training program, you will be considered for such training on a priority basis determined by the scores on which you were originally qualified.

5. You are to be commended for the excellent spirit you have exhibited. Your on-the-line services up to this time in the continental establishments have been an extremely valuable asset to the training program. Your further services with the Air Forces and your future responsibilities in prosecuting the war against Japan will be heavy, for you probably will be scheduled to replace the combat personnel who have served a tour of duty overseas. Wherever you may be assigned you will have the opportunity to contribute actively to the defeat of Japan. Thus, it is my sincere belief that your future service with the Air Forces will be a source of pride both to you and to your country.

6. I have directed that this letter be presented to you in recognition of your expressed willingness and desire to perform combat duties in the air. We have a big job ahead for you in the battles yet to be fought. We are indeed fortunate to have your youth, your intelligence, your courage, and your enthusiasm to do a job for the Army Air Forces and your country. We expect you will do the job wherever it may be your privilege to serve.

B. K. YOUNT
Lieutenant General, USA
Commanding

Contents

List of Illustrations

Fig.5   Primary Flight Instructor & students

Chapter I: The Early Years

UNITED STATES ARMY RECEPTION CENTER
FORT MACARTHUR, SAN PEDRO, CA
JULY 1, 1944

On July 1, 1944 I was transferred from the Ninth Service Command, Fort Douglas, Utah to Fort Mac Arthur which was located in the San Pedro Harbor. The thing I remember most was the huge cannon they had that had to be rolled out on rails to fire. They claimed that the last time they fired it all the windows for some distance were shattered. It was exercised, though, while we were there. My mother and I had a disagreement of some sort just as I was to report to active duty at the Fort. Therefore, I had to resort to riding the "Big Red Streetcar" - the Pacific Electric Railway from Hollywood Boulevard, where my father's office was located to Los Angeles, and then transfer to the train into the Fort area. We only stayed long enough to have haircuts and be fitted with uniforms and then we shipped out via the same type of streetcar to the Los Angeles Union Station for transfer to a train to Amarillo AAFB, for basic training. My parents and my brother Skip and my sister Jeanie came down to see me off, and of course all the guys were interested in meeting Jeanie.

Blow It Out Your...

The second day we were in the Army, an orderly or someone in authority called over an interphone into the barracks we were in to shut up and go to sleep. Unknown to us the interphone went two ways, and when some one yelled "Blow it out your ass!" we were destined for Kitchen Police (KP) on the Fourth of July.

AMARILLO AAFB, AMARILLO, TX
JULY – SEPTEMBER 1944

We arrived in Amarillo in the middle of July for six weeks of basic military training. Our unit consisted of about one third from the Los Angeles area, one third from the Salt Lake City area, and the other third from Baton Rouge, LA. What a mix! This is where I first met Bill Clark, the baddest cuss this side of the Mississippi.

We later became good friends. Clark finished flight training after the war and flew combat in Korea, and later went on to become a Captain with TWA.

While we were in basic training, the young 18-year-old future pilots, navigators and bombardiers were trying to find their place in the unit. There were the inevitable near fights over very silly things, but without much real animosity, even though there was quite a difference in our backgrounds. We were bunked by alphabetical order so Bill Clark was always in the bunk above me or in the one next to me—and a constant pain in the ass throughout the six weeks we were at Amarillo.

"I'm going to kill you, Clark"

During basic training we pulled a 24-hour guard duty; four on, four off. Bill Clark, my nemesis, put shoe polish around the edge of my boots while I was asleep and set it on fire. Both of my feet were blistered all around the edges.

The Monkey, he got drunk

Bill Clark nicknamed me "Monk", mainly because I had hair on my chest and body, and everyone in the outfit called me that for a long time. He used to sing a song, which at the time I had never heard. It was popular during the Spanish American War time:

> "I went to the animal fair,
> The birds and the beasts were there,
> The big baboon by the light of the moon
> Was combing his auburn hair…
>
> The monkey, he got drunk
> and sat on the elephant's trunk.
>
> The elephant sneezed and fell on his knees,
> And that was the end of the monk, the monk…
> That was the end of the monk."

In relating this song in Homeland, John Jakes wrote that the people listening to this refrain at the hotel in Tampa Florida got very tired of it. So did the guys in our barracks, because Clark kept singing it over and over.

Italian Prisoners of War (POWs)

The Italian Prisoners of War (POWs) arrived about halfway through our basic training session. The American military prisoners were moved out of the wooden barracks building jail into sub-standard quarters. The POWs took over the relatively nice quarters. They worked in the Officer's Mess and cooked their own food and had rations of wine and beer.

Once in a while one of the prisoners would decide to leave. When he was caught and brought back nothing was done to him. The Americans took the ration of wine away from all the prisoners. Not many tried to leave after that.

Hey, Greek, help me!

I do not know exactly what this trainee yelled at the cook of Greek origin, but it worked. The trainee had been caught taking water that was off-limits while we were on a march and bivouac. The sentence was to dig a 6x6x6 foot hole in the bottom of the creek bed we were camped next to. Of course it was an impossible job because the sand kept falling back in the hole. The trainee saw this cook on the shore and yelled at him, and the next thing we knew the guy was eating ice cold watermelon in the cook tent.

It was hard for us to believe that when we had finished basic training and were to be moved to a base for "On-the Line-Training", that our destination was such a secret. We did not know even after several days on the troop train where we were going.

Troop Train to Marfa AAFB

The troop cars looked like those we saw in pictures from WWI. They were short ugly looking things. We slept on 3-deck bunks with only a pillow and mattress cover. There were two or three cars and a baggage-type car, which served as a field kitchen. We were herded to the far end of this baggage-kitchen car and given rations to take back to our car. We were routed from Amarillo through Austin, and San Antonio, traveling on land grant railroad tracks to avoid the expense of paying the railroad for our trip. We sat in rail yards and shunts waiting for trains to hook up with our cars. After about four days we arrived in San Antonio, it was

Sunday and they let us loose for several hours. When it was time to return to the train to continue our odyssey, it not surprising that most of the 18-year-old "soldiers" were inebriated. However, several did not make the departure. They had no idea where we were going so they had to seek help. We traveled west from San Antonio up into the Davis Mountains and stopped. There were no buildings or anything. After awhile a number of Burma trucks (short, low-profile personnel carriers) arrived and took us to Marfa AAFB.

USAAF ADVANCED PILOT SCHOOL
3025TH ARMY AIR FORCE BASE UNIT
MARFA AAFB, MARFA, TEXAS
SEPTEMBER 1944—MARCH 1945

The Marfa Army Air Force Base at Marfa Texas was located about midway between Marfa and Alpine in the Davis Mountains. The mission of the base was advanced multi-engine pilot training. The attraction at Alpine was girls. The Sol Ross College was located there, and of course most of the student body consisted of girls. Most of us tried to stay "clean" of demerits so we could get a Saturday afternoon and evening in Alpine. Not Bill Clark, he never got a pass the entire time we knew him.

The Army had overestimated the casualty rate among aircrews and the duration of the hostilities, therefore they recruited too many potential pilots, navigators and bombardiers. They screened and re-screened the pool of aircrew trainees. We were what were left and they were reluctant to release us from the possible pipeline until it was clear the war was nearly over. Therefore the pool was split between several pilot-training bases and we were called "On-the-Line-Trainees". We were not allowed to participate in much real training or drive vehicles. We lived under aviation cadet rules and had our own student officers.

Here come the Inspecting Officers

Bill Clark's favorite trick was to throw a bottle of neosyneferin in the red-hot pot-belly stove just as the inspecting party opened the barracks door. It would explode and send soot all over that end of the barracks.

Fig 6   Recognition of 500 hours of flight instruction

No respect for student officer authority

One of the punishments meted out to those who couldn't or wouldn't behave in a proper manner was Saturday morning "awkward squad". A student officer would conduct several hours of close order drill of recalcitrant soldiers with rifles and in class A uniforms. Clark had a lot of trouble with this and finally burst out with a challenge to the student officer conducting the drill. He was sort of a prissy kind of guy, and Clark felt it would feel good to go to the gym, put the gloves on and beat the hell out of this guy. This was all under the guidance of the boxing coach. When Clark returned to the barracks he looked like he had been dragged through a bramble bush. The "prissy" student officer's father had sent him to the YMCA when he was a kid and he really learned to box. He beat the hell out of Clark. Clark was careful with his challenges after that.

> One job we were assigned was to go with the permanent party soldiers at Marfa to pick up the laundry from Fort D. A. Russell. We all enjoyed this trip and we were able to observe the mighty Afrika Corps at work. They were a good-looking bunch of guys and they did not seem to mind doing the laundry. In fact I imagine many of them returned to the States after the war was over.

German POWs Worked the Laundry

German POWs at Fort D. A. Russell in Marfa did all the laundry for our base. This was an old army base used by General Pershing to chase Pancho Villa during the Mexican fracas. The German officers ran the laundry and most of the prisoners were from the Afrika Corps. Security was really minimal. It consisted of one American soldier with a rifle and helmet liner lying on the grass sleeping, outside the laundry building, and one other soldier at the front gate. The Germans drove all vehicles on the base and were not contained at all. When a German decided to leave, he was usually caught and returned very quickly and all beer rations removed for a week. Not many Germans wanted to leave.

> I learned early that if you kept your head down and didn't make a lot of noise over small things you could do mostly whatever you wanted. I took

*advantage of the training I had received in high school and the two
semesters I spent at Parks Air College prior to being called to active duty.*

Worked half days—had Squadron and Weather Office confused

When we were assigned to Marfa we were to get some training
being around airplanes. Most of the unit was wakened at 0500 to
be ready to go on the flight line by 0600. It was cold and some
times very wet. The On-the-Line Trainees (OLTs) fueled the
twin-engine trainers and washed windshields for the morning
flights. I wangled a job in the base weather office that started at
0900 since I could read the hourly reports, construct them and do
balloon observations. This let the GI weather observers goof off
more so they were good instructors. They were particularly happy
with me when I did the piball routine. The squadron I was in
thought I worked there all day, and weather office thought I had
to be back in the squadron in the afternoon.*

"Make my bed and mop—or I'll squeal on you"

The guys living near me were somewhat envious of my "bankers"
hours told me that if I didn't make their beds and mop the entire
area each day they were going to squeal on me. So I did.

"We'll excuse you from further classes"

The sergeant teaching engines class was not too bright and I had
just finished a year of engines at Parks Air College and couldn't
keep my mouth shut, and was always correcting his mistakes. The
Squadron Sergeant told me not to attend the classes anymore, but
didn't give me anything else to do.

"Don't You Work in Base Security?"

John Long was the stoolie in the Squadron for Security, and most
of us at least suspected it. Long and I were hitching a ride back to
the base from the city of Marfa one night and a person in civilian

---

*Releasing a balloon and tracking it with a theodolite until you could no
longer see it with the instrument obtained the pilot balloon (piball)
reports. The winters were cold and blustery so having this kid out there
doing their job was greatly appreciated by the observers.

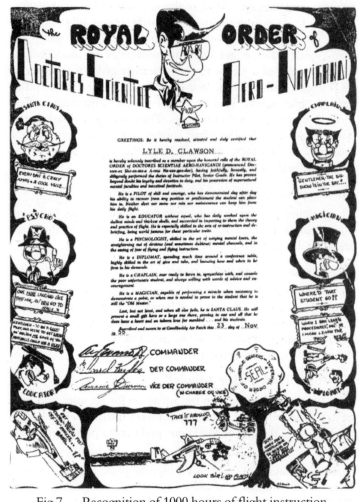

Fig.7 Recognition of 1000 hours of flight instruction

clothing picked us up. He had his wife in the car and Long started mumbling and he was afraid he would say something offensive that his wife would hear. I explained that it was unlikely he would say anything bad, and about that time Long leaned forward and said he thought he knew him, didn't he work in security? Long said that was the last time he heard from security.

Mess Hall Sergeant to OLT – "Sit over there!"

Bill Clark was late to eat lunch one day and the Mess Sergeant told him not to sit in the area that had been cleaned, but sit in a messy area, in the sun. Clark threw a jam jar top at him and told him to go to hell. Before this happened Clark had so many demerits that he never got to go to town. They eliminated him from the aircrew-training program, and then a couple of days later reinstated him. He was free of all demerits, but still got enough new ones that he never made a pass the following weekend.

> More to keep us busy than any training benefit we were required to participate in repetitious activities such as close order drill, physical training and the favorite of all, frequent Kitchen Police, (KP).

"Cut my finger, cut my finger," Clark—"Cut your own"

Bill Clark was among about ten guys from our flight detailed to eye and finish preparing 35-gallon cans of potatoes for the mess halls. We were in what had been the bakery. There were other activities in the hall and there was a Sergeant in charge of us, but he was in another room. Clark accidentally cut his finger and went to get a band-aid. When he came back he went in another room and got his coat and started putting it on. One gullible character asked him what he was doing. He said that with his cut finger he wasn't allowed to help prepare the potatoes. The guy then begged Clark to cut his finger so he could go with him; Clark's response was, "Cut your own finger!". The guy took several swipes with his eyes closed and finally damn near cut his finger off. He went for the band-aid and asked the Sergeant if he was released now. Of course the Sergeant told him to get out there and quit goofing off. When he went out, Clark was eyeing the potatoes, and once again got threatened with mayhem.

Boxing = Bloody Nose

I was in the boxing group and when I got into the ring I invariably ended up with a bloody nose. This would get me out of the afternoon parade. Bill Clark got a bottle of red ink, put it on a handkerchief and would apply it to his nose and hold it. They would go get the student officer in charge and try to get Clark out of the parade also. Sometimes it worked, others he got another demerit for cheating.

> *Having grown up in a very rural North Hollywood, California, I was not exposed to a great deal of ethnic minority problems. The Mexican families lived in the eastern side of the community and we did not have much contact with them. The Mexicans and Japanese worked in agriculture and seemed to be happy with their circumstances. I do not remember many problems at school that could be traced to ethnic difficulties. There were no black students in any school that I attended. I don't know if this was by design or that they just didn't live in the areas. So when I first encountered segregation it was disgusting to me. But, as shown by my stupid remarks below, I acquired some of this racial bias after a while.*

My first racial problem encounter

The black soldiers at Marfa were housed separately had their own BX, with no Officers club and worked at menial tasks. The black soldiers working in the Mess Hall took a lot of guff from the Southern boys and one day after a nasty remark by one of the white OLTs, the black soldier came over the steam table with a BIG knife and had to be restrained. They were treated like animals and it gave me a rotten taste in my mouth.

My Second Encounter With My Own Attitude about Race.

Long and I were making a nuisance of ourselves in Alpine, a town just to the east of Marfa, one Saturday night and the Military Police (MPs) chased Long and me over a train, caught us, and put us on a bus back to the base. En route an MP truck stopped the bus and put two black soldiers on it. When they exited the MP truck, old big mouth with too much beer inside (me) said out loud something about stopping the bus for a couple of "niggars". Lights on in the bus, it was full of black soldiers, and Long and I were the only white guys on the bus! Damn near got killed, but a big black Master Sergeant intervened, and I never said anything like that again in my life.

When it was apparent that we were not needed as aircrew trainees, which was very costly, we were sent back to Amarillo Army Air Force Base. We still had not been totally released yet so we still drew menial tasks. The primary mission of the base was to train newly commissioned pilots to be B-29 flight engineers. They received ground school and simulator training at Amarillo and then were sent to Hondo Army Air Force Base for flight training. Needless to say the young pilots were very upset about this turn of events and many choose to quit flying and faced Flying Evaluation Board action. Many of them were grounded and some released from active duty.

"You're at Hangar Six Tech Order Library"

Peggy was our secretary in the section I was assigned as a Technical Order Librarian. She was also the niece of a cowboy movie star named Big Boy Williams. He lived about a mile from me in North Hollywood and Peggy had visited him there so she knew just where I lived. I liked her a lot, but she must have been two years older than me. The librarian job was an impossible task and therefore, being young and crooked, I dodged it carefully. There were six big hangars on the flight line and each of them had at least one large Tech Order Library. I used to goof off and seldom did much work. Peggy would call our squadron orderly room and ask a runner to go to my barracks and she would tell where she had sent the Captain to look for me. I would get dressed quickly and go to the spot. I never got caught goofing off like that.

"Salute that big black Buick"

Bud Barrett had been assigned to the MP Squadron and gave a ticket to a big black Buick for a parking violation at the BX. It was the Major General's car and his wife was being chauffeured in it. Bud knew exactly what he was doing and relished the excitement.

The MP commander really gave him hell.

Roll me over in the clover and do it again

Each month the Hospital Commander would award a large red flag with a big white VD on it to the Squadron Commander that had the highest VD rate in the Wing. This was done by having a small, but loud band playing the title song and marching from the previous Squadron to present the flag to the new champion

Hitch-hiking on a Greyhound Bus

Some way I wangled a three-day pass and hitch hiked to Denver for a short vacation. I contacted the father of a fellow I went to Occidental College with, who was an attorney. He had me to his house for dinner and then asked a nice young lady he knew if she would like to go to the big amusement park in Denver. We had a nice time, rode the streetcar back to her house and I stayed at the YMCA. When my pass was about up I started back to Amarillo. In Pueblo, Colorado, I was sitting alongside the road at night trying to get a ride. A Greyhound Bus stopped and allowed me on without paying. I sat in the jump seat next to the driver and we chatted all the way into Amarillo. He said he wouldn't have stopped for me, but his whole bus was full of soldiers, so he figured there were no spotters on the bus.

He looks dead

For some reason we were standing down in the barracks one day and someone shouted out that a soldier lying on his bed looked very strange. He was not moving and did not respond to questions. We at first thought he was dead, because his eyes were wide open. Eventually he spoke to us and said he usually slept with his eyes open, and this had previously caused concern about his condition.

> Sometime in February, 1945, the decision was made to send the balance of the OLTs to technical training. The war against the Japanese was not over and there evidently was a need for various technical skills to man bombers. I was in a group selected for radio operator-mechanic school at Scott AAFB in outside of Bellville, Illinois.

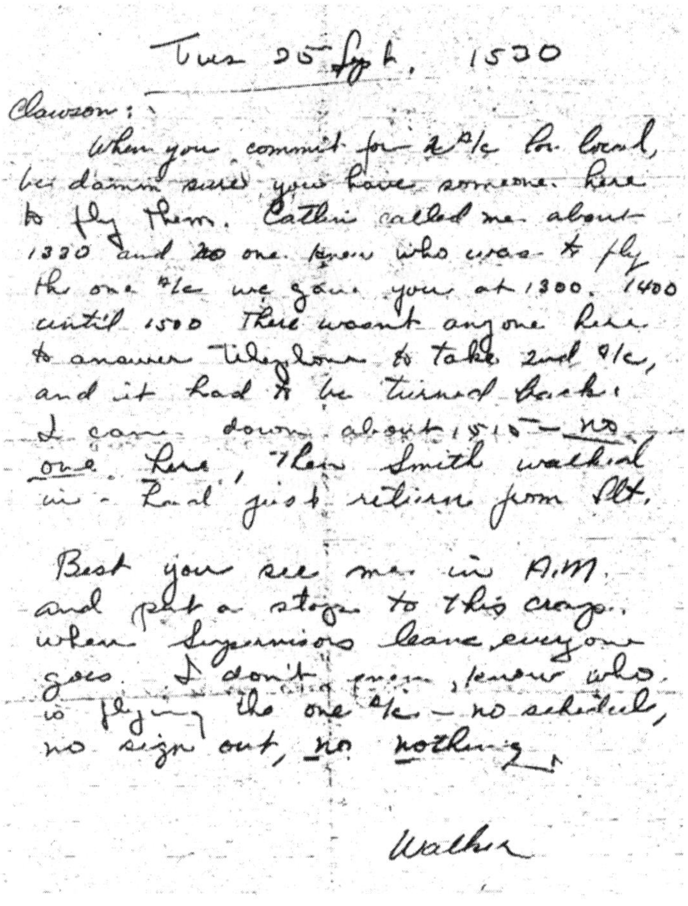

Tues 25 Sept. 1500

Clawson:—

When you commit for 2½ hr. local,
be damn sure you have someone here
to fly them. Cathie called me about
1330 and no one knew who was to fly
the one a/c we gave you at 1300. 1400
until 1500 There wasn't anyone here
to answer telephone to take 2nd a/c,
and it had to be turned back.
I came down about 1510 — no
one here. Then Smith walked
in — had just returned from flt.

Best you see me in A.M.
and put a stop to this crap.
When Supervisors leave everyone
goes. I don't even know who
is flying the one a/c — no schedule,
no sign out, no nothing.

                                    Walker

Fig.8   Captain Walker's Missive

3505TH ARMY AIR FORCE TSS UNIT
SCOTT AAFB, BELLVILLE, ILLINOIS
JULY 14, 1945—AUGUST 11, 1945

Scott Field, as the locals knew the base, was a large technical training school. Many technical skills were taught here. It was one of the oldest of the Army Air Corps bases and had many permanent buildings as well as the temporary WWII barracks.

Twenty-five hours of logged flying time

When it was apparent the Air Force had no need for more aircrew trainees, we were shipped off to various technical schools. I was sent to Scott AAFB to radio mechanic/operator school along with a number of my On-the-Line trainees [OLT] compatriots. We really did not do well and the morale was terrible. One day shortly after we arrived a fellow came by and said, "Don't you have twenty-five hours flying time logged?" I did, and was selected for training at the Liaison Pilot School at Sheppard AAFB. The woman Second Lieutenant who was the recorder for the selection board chewed me out for not having my Private First Class stripe sewn on my uniform. I never did wear them.

3706TH ARMY AIR FORCE BASE UNIT
(BASIC TRAINING CENTER AND PILOT SCHOOL)
SHEPPARD AAFB, WICHITA FALLS, TEXAS
AUGUST 11, 1945—OCTOBER 28, 1945

"This individual has been honorably discharged for the Convenience of the Government and will be acceptable for future military service if presented for induction by Selective Service."

This was a notation placed on our discharges. When I signed up for the draft after I returned to North Hollywood, the draft board secretary said they were going to draft me again. I said "Never!". I was married February 1, 1946.

Hitch-hiking, picked up by old man in Model T

Once while stationed at Sheppard Field after the war was over, I hitch hiked to Amarillo to see some of my friends. I was on my way back and I was out in the barren lands of Texas in the middle of the night, when this old man in a Model T truck with no cab, just a buckboard type seat stopped and picked me up. Another soldier was in the passenger seat, and as the truck would start up a hill the lights would dim to almost out and the old man would slowly start to run off the road. The soldier next to me would just reach up and steer the truck back on the road. The truck had a flatbed on the back and until we reached a little town and stopped. I didn't notice until then that there must have been six or more soldiers passed out on the truck bed. No one said much of anything the whole time I was on the vehicle. It was really weird.

The night of the announcement that the war was over was wild. Rolls and rolls of toilet paper were thrown over the telephone lines and set on fire. One of the Woman Army Corps' (WAC's) barracks was burned and all hell broke loose for a while. After that there was very little serious attention to soldiering.

Only Furlough: started early—ended late

We were given an opportunity to take a furlough, as we thought we were going to be shipped overseas to replace people who had been in longer than we had been. I worked in the Air Inspector's office as a technical order clerk and told the officer in charge I was going on furlough, and left. Of course it was about three days before I actually got my furlough papers. I hitch-hiked to Amarillo, Texas, got my friend who worked in an orderly room to make up some furlough papers, hitch-hiked on a B-25 going to Edwards AAFB in California, and arrived home two days before my furlough started. A friend picked up my real furlough papers and mailed them to me. I obtained an extension and went back a week late. I went to the Los Angeles Train Station and could not get on the train and it was packed. The stationmaster wrote me a note saying so, and I tried it again the next day. The stationmaster recognized me and when he gave me the second note, told me to get there early the next day because he would not give me another note. On he train I met a fellow from my outfit who had been absent without official leave (AWOL) in Los Angeles for a month, but his first sergeant knew where he was, said the sergeant called him and told him to get back, we were being discharged.

Fig.9   Flight Commander and "Staff"

I was discharged on October 28, 1945 with approximately 15 months of active duty. Someone had made the decision that since we had enlisted directly into the Army Air Forces for aircrew training, and Government had not provided the training, we were entitled to be discharged. Therefore the following statement appears on my discharge:

> This individual has been honorably discharged for the Convenience of the Government and will be acceptable for future military service if presented for induction by Selective Service.

This was a notation placed on our discharges. When I signed up for the draft after I returned to North Hollywood, the draft board secretary said they were going to draft me again. I said *never*, and on February 1, 1946, I got married.

Bus to Amarillo Ran Out of Gas

When we were discharged and received our "Ruptured Duck" insignia on our uniforms, Roland Darby from North Hollywood and I started hitch-hiking to Amarillo to use Highway 66 into LA. We caught several rides, but ended up in the boonies so decided to buy tickets on the next bus to come through. It was full of discharged soldiers and a few girls. We traveled a distance and then out in nowhere: the bus ran out of gas. By the time they got more gas everyone on the bus was crocked.

Although the following discussion of the US Weather Bureau has no relevance to my military activities, it provided the impetus for pursuing the direct commission, which would allow me to apply for flying training.

US WEATHER BUREAU, FLAGSTAFF, ARIZONA
OCTOBER 1947-FEBRUARY 1948

After finishing college in September, 1947 I accepted a job with the US Weather Bureau in Flagstaff, Arizona. During that time I worked on obtaining a direct commission in the Air Force. I had intended to return to flying training as soon as I could. My father had been in the Air Service during the First World War and had very little good to say about the service and the people in it. He persuaded me to enter business with him until

1953, when I did volunteer and was accepted for pilot training.

Interview at Williams AFB for Direct Commission

During the interview with the Board of Officers there was a discussion regarding the racial issue of whether blacks should be integrated completely or given separate and equal facilities and opportunities. I related an experience I had had at Marfa AAFB wherein a Southern white soldier make a degrading remark to one of the black soldiers working the steam table giving out food. The black soldier came over the top of the steam table with a knife. Both parties were restrained and no one was injured. I felt, with my very limited experience, that integration was not going to be possible for many years to come, if ever. I truthfully believed that separate and equal was the only answer. I received my direct commission in the reserve.

UNITED STATES AIR FORCE

PRIMARY FLIGHT SCHOOL

BAINBRIDGE AIR BASE, BAINBRIDGE, GEORGIA

JANUARY—JULY 1953

Bainbridge Air Base was a civilian contract school in that all of the instructors both ground and flight were civilians. The base was under the command of a lieutenant colonel and there were several Air Force check pilots.

I was called to active duty from the reserves in the grade of First Lieutenant to go to pilot school. I was 26 years old and had three children. We flew Piper Cubs and T-6 aircraft and went to ground school throughout the course of training. I was assigned to Bainbridge AB. At Parks Air College I had qualified for a private pilot's license, so the Cub presented little or no challenge. That T-6 was different. Once they put the hood on me I had all the challenge I could use.

Bainbridge AB was located just north of Tallahassee, Florida. Most if not all of the instructors were former army or Navy pilots from WWII. The Base Commander was a Lt. Col. His wife was an Army Brat, big mouth and all. Upon hearing that her husband was to be transferred, and thinking it would be very soon, she went around town and told all the civilian bigwigs what she thought of them. Her husband's orders were canceled and they had to stay months longer. Naturally she couldn't show her face in town.

Fig.10   SAC crew number E-60

Request Change of Instructors

We were told in the orientation session before starting training that if we were not failing any flying lesson and felt we wanted a change of instructors, we would be accommodated. My first instructor had been a crop duster after leaving the Army. He spent most of each session chasing wispy smoke coming out of the piney woods and pulling as many 'Gs" as he could to see if I would black out. After a couple of sessions of this, I went to the flight commander and asked for change of instructors. Of course he badgered me to tell why. I wouldn't, and reminded him of the orientation speech he had given. He still pestered me for quiet awhile to tell him. I never did.

Minimum Fuel, Request no Go-around

After I had soloed the T-6, I flew a mission with my instructor and after an hour or so he said to land and he would get out and I was to go back up and practice spins for a specified period. I did, and when I was returning to the base I could hear that runway control was in rare form and sending many of the approaching airplanes around because of some discrepancy in their approach. I noted that my fuel was sufficient for a landing, but if I had to go around, I might be low. I requested no go-around due to fuel state. I was cleared to land and then the civilian flight commander jumped all over me. I told him I had done just what my instructor had told me to do but that the next time I'd keep my mouth shut and if I ran out of fuel, I'd just bail out. He gave up.

Although we had several foreign nations represented in the student body of our class, only the Danes performed well. Most if not all of the other countries' students were eliminated in training for flying deficiencies. The Danes were really good pilots and quick-witted, as shown in the following story.

"Act like you're sleepwalking"

We had several different foreign national students. The ones that were the most fun were the Danes. Two of them met two girls who were sisters and went on a date with them. They ended up going to dinner with them at the girls' home. Their parents were most cordial to them and when they had finished dinner it was late and they lived some distance from the Base. The parents invited them to spend the night. Well, one of those Danes took it his head to try to get into his girls' room in the middle of the night. She was frightened and screamed; her parents and the other Dane come running. The running Dane, thinking very fast now, said in Danish, "Act like you're sleepwalking". It worked.

UNITED STATES AIR FORCE
BASIC FLIGHT SCHOOL
REESE AFB, LUBBOCK, TEXAS,
JULY 1953—JANUARY 1954

Reese Air Force Base was an undergraduate multi-engine flight training base under the Air Force Training Command. Students flew the T-28 for a short time, concentrating on instrument training, and then went into the B-25. The officers were given their wings here and rated as airplane pilots. The aviation cadets were commissioned and rated here also. When I completed my training I was assigned to Goodfellow AFB, at San Angelo, Texas, as an instructor in B-25 aircraft.

"Major, what does the acronym 'DNIF' mean?"

Our instructor in B-25s at Reese was a WWII veteran and really an old salt. He thought for a minute and said that he really didn't know what the letters meant, but some thought it stood for "Drunk, not interested in flying". This was sort of typical of many of the people in the service. The actual meaning of letters was not known as well as the result. These letters actually meant "Duty not involving flying".

Shoot another Flare

I had just cleared the active runway on a solo flight with another student pilot and we saw the B-25 following us in the pattern start his flare to land. The thing that caught our attention was a number of flares being fired from runway control and a lot of chatter on the radio telling the pilot that the landing gear was not down. The landing was almost perfect except for that. It was a Friday afternoon and the flying safety officer and many other senior officers were gone for the weekend, so the aircraft, sans gear, sat on the runway all weekend.

UNITED STATES AIR FORCE
INSTRUCTOR FLIGHT SCHOOL
CRAIG AFB, SELMA, ALABAMA, JAN—MAR 1954

Before we could instruct students at Goodfellow AFB we all had to attend the Air Force Instructor School at Selma, Alabama. We flew North American T-28s in training. There were also T-33s and T-6s used for training at the school. When we finished the course, our check ride was to give a lesson to an instructor who was in the front seat.

That's the way he always flies

My new friend, 2nd Lt. John Newsom, gave an instructor a lesson and came back telling our instructor how he had yelled at this guy for all the wild things he tried. John thought the instructor was just testing him, but our instructor told John that what he had experienced was the way the guy flew all the time.

Crash! "I can't see a thing." Norwegian AF pilot

There was a Norwegian AF pilot attending the instructor school on an exchange basis. He had flown some pretty hot English fighters and was quite experienced. He was practicing instruments in the back seat when all of sudden I heard this loud crash. He had bottomed out his seat and the hood came down and he said, "Don, you had better take control—I can't see a thing!"

Son Charlie and Joe d'bull

My oldest son Charlie was 4½ years old in Selma and we lived in an apartment on a farm outside of town. There was a corral right next to our apartment in which they kept a big old bull. Charlie's favorite pastime was crawling through the fence and seeing if he could run across the corral before Joe d'bull could catch him. It was obvious that he had not fallen far from the tree.

We were on Temporary Duty at Craig AFB for the school, so when we had completed the training we returned to San Angelo, and spent a wonderful three years teaching kids to fly the B-25.

40

Chapter II: United States Air Force Basic Flight School

3546TH PILOT TRAINING SQUADRON
GOODFELLOW AFB, SAN ANGELO, TEXAS
MARCH 1954—JANUARY 1957

At the time I was assigned to Goodfellow it was operating primarily as the only Air Force operated primary flying school in the Air Force. There were many T-6 Texan aircraft at the base when I arrived. There were very few B-25s at this time and hardly any students or instructors in the B-25 school. The new instructors were the most current in the B-25. The student load was quite heavy for a while. Most of us had eight students, which was almost impossible to handle. It wasn't long until we were properly staffed and then the student load was about four to an instructor.

I was very pleased with my assignment as a flight instructor in this very new B-25 school. Goodfellow had long been a T-6 primary school, but was transitioning into the B-25s. Captain Jim Prather was my first flight commander. He was rough as a cob, a no-nonsense officer from Texas. He was even a mean-looking guy. He got into lots of trouble from time to time for calling the students little "piss-pants" and worse.

This Officer only participates in Official Duties

Major Krafka, my reporting officer, stated in my officer effectiveness report (OER) that "this officer only participates in official duties and not in the various extra-curriculum baseball games and parties". I had missed one baseball game, due to family problems, and normally went to everything. From that time on whenever we had a function, I always made it a point to look him up and tell him I made this one. After a while he said to stop and promised that he would never make another statement such as that in anyone's OER.

Captain Jim Prather was a good guy to work for because you always knew where you stood with him. If you did something stupid, you could expect a good chewing out such as only a Texan can provide. He used to raise hell

Fig. 11   B-47 refueling with KC-97

with the students in a group several times a week. He would rant and call them some typical lowlife names because it appeared to him that they were not taking the training serious enough. The newly appointed Second Lieutenants from ROTC still had the draft hanging over them if they washed out of pilot school and were not recommended for other aircrew training.

"Which one of you little piss-ants...?"

One event that was memorable was when one or more of the students took exception to having their ancestors categorized as lowlifes went to Colonel Alexander Evanoff, the Training Group Commander, and complained. Colonel Evanoff felt compelled to invite Captain Prather to a good old-fashioned ass-chewing. When he had finished, Jim went back to the flight shack, called a meeting of all of the students and started of with, "Which one of you little piss-ants went to Colonel Evanoff and filled him with all those lies?" The students finally just gave up and took Jim's counseling in silence.

"Trespass and Conversion—What the hell is this?"

One Friday night at the O'Club, the Group Commander, Colonel Evanoff grabbed me and dragged me into the club officer's office and started yelling at me about "What the hell is this, trespassing and conversion?". Seems the fellow who had been pestering my father and me about having bought lumber from a sawmill in California before I returned to active duty wrote to Air Force Headquarters wanting to know when Lieutenant Clawson would be available for a trial. He was claiming that because we had bought lumber from a mill that had a contract to log the land this fellow owned and was in Chapter 11 of the Bankruptcy Act, that we had trespassed on his property, taken lumber and converted it into sales and cash. I had a helluva time convincing Evanoff that I had not committed a serious crime.

"Tell him to sue me, just like any other homeowner"

When we moved into the rental house in San Angelo, there was no provision for a clothes washer so I had a plumber give me an estimate for installing the necessary plumbing. When he finished he wanted about twice as much as he had bid. I wouldn't pay him until he gave me a bill for the amount we had agreed it was to cost. A Master Sergeant from the base was a good friend of the plumber and came to our flight shack and told me I had to pay the bill the plumber had given me. The Sergeant said if I didn't pay, he was going to talk to my commander. I told him I had already explained my problem to my commander and if the plumber felt he had a case, to sue me, just as he would do with a civilian. I received a revised bill and paid it right away. I also told the Sergeant that he was way out of line and if I ever heard of him doing that again, I would go to his commander.

Now they're in the handball courts

Since I did not have enough flying time to be aerodrome officer, I was occasionally detailed to Officer of the Day. Here is where you find out what goes on with the troops. One night I was called by the Air Police and told to come to the handball courts on the base. These were lockable from the inside to keep intruders out when a game was in progress. It also worked for airmen and girls at night when they were looking for privacy. The Air Police used to try to keep them open at night, with little or no success. That night several were in use, and I told the cops to go do something else.

"She's not in here, Sergeant"

The same night an AP saw a young women going into a barracks after dark and followed her in. He could not find her until all the wall lockers were opened, and there she was. She lived next door to the First Sergeant of the APs and worked for a newspaper in town. Nothing more was said about it.

Air Force JAG in back seat, T-28

A young attorney from the Judge Advocate's Office at Goodfellow, a Lieutenant, lived next door to us in town. He had not flown any air force aircraft before and so I made arrangements for a T-28 for a proficiency flight one Saturday morning. There was about a five thousand foot overcast over the base and we filed an instrument flight plan and flew a round-robin to Fort Worth, Waco and back to San Angelo. Shortly after take-off I realized that there was a rudder trim problem of some sort, and I had to use too much trim to offset the thrust. I reported this on the way back, and we started a let down. There wasn't much conversation between cockpits, because I was somewhat busy with the aircraft problem and air traffic control. When we broke clear of the clouds at about 5,000', I did a roll for some cockamamie reason, clearly not being considerate of my passenger. We then proceeded to make turns so that an airborne C-47 on a maintenance check flight could observe our rudder, thus putting him in near proximity of our airplane.

When all this was over and we decided that I would make a normal landing, we made the approach and the runway was lined with fire engines and ambulances. After an uneventful landing and taxi in, the prissy Flying Safety Officer jumped up on the wing and I opened the canopy, my young attorney handed him his flight cap, which was full. He had up chucked several times, evidently, not saying a word. The prissy one almost did the same and threw the hat on the ramp. The attorney never asked to go again.

Shut off Fuel—C-47

I was checked out in the base C-47 and from time to time flew extra missions. We departed Goodfellow very early one Sunday morning to fly to McClellan AFB in Sacramento for a much needed part for one of the B-25s. Everyone was pretty well bedded down except the pilots when we crossed Tucson. It was time to change the source of fuel for the port engine. I was in the pilot seat so made the selection. Obviously not too awake myself, I selected OFF and it wasn't long until everyone was wide-awake since the port engine quit. We were alert enough to retard the throttle before restoring fuel flow to the engine and restarting it.

Mountain Wave Effect

To add some realism to the training program I set out to take my students to Oxnard AFB, California using oxygen to allow us to fly at about 16,000 feet. There were only two or three B-25s on the base that had an operating O_2 system but we were able to get one. The mountains from El Paso to Tucson run pretty much north and south, so as we approached a range of mountains our airspeed would start to fall off, requiring high blower and almost full power to keep the airspeed in a safe range, As we passed over the range the airspeed would build up and pretty soon we were hauling the power off again. This happened several times so we knew it was not the airplane. We also knew that we had a direct headwind of about 80 knots. When we arrived at Williams AFB in Arizona, the first thing I did was go into the weather office and asked the forecaster what the heck we had been up against. As soon as I told him the story he said that we had encountered mountain waves. No one had ever mentioned such a thing in the weather classes I had taken both in the Air Force and at Parks College.

The base operations people were concerned because they had a C-47 overdue with a general officer on board. We told them that we had seen the Gooney Bird way below us, but also fighting the headwind. The airplane arrived while we were still in base ops.

Don't look out—get on instruments

A student crew and I were flying in a B-25 over the San Joaquin Valley one night on our way to Sacramento, California, when I noticed that it appeared the ground lights were in the sky and vice versa. I knew right away that I had vertigo and alerted the crew not to look out and get on the instruments and stay on them. We had no autopilots on most of the B-25s so it was necessary to hand fly the airplane all of the time. This made it extremely difficult if you didn't recognize this type of situation and rely on the instruments. One guy had a peek—and sure enough he damn near panicked.

Does this complete your mission?

Lt. John Newsom and I were flying a single-engine T-28 in the local area just for fun. We started shooting touch and goes, I was in the back seat and John had just started a take-off after rolling a short distance down the runway. We got to about 500' and the engine quit. Now, we were always told to land straight ahead if we lost an engine on take-off., but John wasn't having any of that. He started a turn back to our take-off runway reciprocal of about 030 degrees, when he saw that he could make the north runway and told me to tell the tower that we would be landing north. They came back with, "Negative, that runway has just had its numbers repainted and they are wet." We didn't even respond, landed on the north runway and as we rolled out, the tower asked if that completed our mission. There we sat on the runway with the propeller straight up and down and they ask a stupid question like that. We had to be towed in.

"Quit screwing around"—T28 over Amarillo

John Newsom and I flew a T-28 to Amarillo so that he could buy an engagement ring for Trudy, his wife to be. We arrived in the afternoon; he flew out to his brother's farm and caught him on a tractor. John made him leave the tractor, we were so low. We went to dinner with his parents, bought the ring, and went back out to the Municipal Airport to leave. It was night and I flew the leg back to Goodfellow. After we leveled off, the engine starting missing, I thought it was John screwing around with the mixture or something like that and blasted him. It turned out the damn engine just about failed. We had more than our share of engine problems with the T-28.

We'll take a GCA into Oxnard AFB—B-25s

The Base Operations Officer at Goodfellow AFB had set up some crazy rules about cross-countries that limited our range to one nautical mile for each hour of flying time the pilot had accumulated to date. This was when we were flying out of Base Ops. When we were flying with students, no limitations were imposed. John Newsom and I wanted to go to the West Coast, but had to take two aircraft and four students in order to go. My radio receiver worked okay, but I couldn't transmit so John made all my calls and we flew a loose formation to Phoenix, refueled and took off for Oxnard AFB, right on the coast. As usual for the time of the year there was lots of fog and low ceilings, so we had to take a GCA in formation. I landed first and John went around and made another GCA and we got to North Hollywood late that night.

He's not flying with my Instructors—B-25

I was Flight Commander of a training flight and as such one of my jobs was to ride with students who were having trouble with their training. I would not let instructors change students around until they had received three consecutive failing grades on flights. Then a supervisor rode an evaluation flight and if it seemed that with more instruction the student had a chance of making it we changed instructors. If they received another three consecutive failing grades, either the deputy flight commander or myself would ride with them. This was considered an elimination ride. The student seldom survived this ride because he had been shown to be unable to grasp the banana and become a reliable pilot. With this in mind, I was to fly with a student who had gone through all of this. The flight went well, he flew a reasonably good traffic pattern and it looked as if he was going to do well. We turned final, full flaps gear down, ready to round out for the landing, and the s. o. b. shoved the stick straight-forward. This woke me up; I grabbed the yoke and pulled back as much as I could in a short time. We landed hard, and taxied in. We were through and he was recommended for elimination. Jake Durnin, a Captain in the Stage section was to ride with him. Jake was kind of a scaredy cat anyway, but he came back, said he did a good job and just needed some good instruction. He said he was putting him back in my flight with a recommendation that he have a change of instructors. I told him that none of my instructors were going to fly with him. Jake then decided that he would instruct him and show us. The next flight he pulled the stick straight-forward trick on him and scared him half to death. He was eliminated.

Change your flight plan

During the time I instructed students in the B-25, we made many extended cross-country flights for training, with the students doing all of the planning and flying. They would be given an outline of the expected outcome of the training, and I would then interject problems and changes as the flight progressed.

Since my parents and many friends lived in the Southern California area, I would direct that many of these flights be made into the Van Nuys or Oxnard, California area. A flight plan would be filed for a stop over at Biggs AFB, in El Paso, Texas, which is right on the Mexican border. After making several simulated instrument approaches to Biggs AFB, I would instruct the student flying that the simulated weather at Biggs had just dropped below minimums for landing, and to file an amended flight plan to Davis–Monthan AFB, a strategic air command base at Tucson, Arizona.

Confusion reigned in the cockpit while the student dug out the charts and books to file the flight plan while all the time the aircraft was headed directly into Mexico. I would offer to fly the airplane, per the student pilots' instructions, while he processed the change. Sometimes, in order to avoid an Air Defense Identification Zone (ADIZ) violation, I would have to make some minor adjustments in the flight path.

Air Traffic Control (ATC) communications were not too efficient at that time, and Davis–Monthan AFB was never notified before our arrival and so we were always greeted with a large contingent of Security Forces, with weapons at the ready. I did this four or five time and we would always be instructed to taxi off the active runway, hold, and shut down the engines. The Air Police would enter the aircraft and we would have to show personal identification and our flight plan. We would then be directed to taxi to a rather remote area for parking and refueling— they never really trusted us.

The primary reason for all of this was not so much that they thought we were terrorists or were intent on doing physical damage, as it was that the Strategic Air Command and Numbered Air Force Headquarters were always dispatching infiltrators to SAC bases to test the security. If they could breach the security, heads would roll and the Air Police responsible were usually shipped to a northern tier base (Montana, North Dakota, Thule) to guard airplanes, such as B-52s, in the winter.

We ain't playing chicken with nobody

I was supervisor of night flying for a solo night flying period. I was in the lead ship with a couple of students and John Newsom was the last aircraft in the stream. We had about seven aircraft between us. We went to Oklahoma City, Fort Worth, Waco, San Antonio and home. Every one returned but one aircraft. We checked with all the airways radios we could and called them on Guard Channel, nothing. We landed and had operations call all the radios en route: nothing. Finally, from our position on the ramp we saw a big red light, which was in the nose of all B-25s, coming from the east. They contacted the tower and made a normal landing. It was two black students. They explained that they came back into the local area and there were red nose lights everywhere, so they turned tail and flew out to the east until there was no more tower traffic and then came into land. Their excuse was that "they weren't going to play chicken with nobody".

How the hell did we get to Midland, Odessa?

We used to take students on a day-night cross-country for training. I had heard other instructors say they would allow the students to run the whole thing on the way home and they would sit in the upper turret. I thought I'd try it and the students flew as pilot and co-pilot. About halfway back I must have drifted off to sleep. When I woke up and went forward to see how we were doing I saw the lights of two larger than expected cities. I recognized them as Midland and Odessa. The students had taken a right turn at Big Springs, Texas instead of a short dog-leg to the south-east! I didn't fly with students again unless I was in one of the pilot's position. We were a good 50-100 miles off course.

Hard landing at Scott Field—C-47.

One of the many trips I made flying the Gooney Bird was to pick up some special services equipment including a couple of pool tables from Sampson AFB, NY The crew chief had not recalculated the weight and balance on the airplane once the pool tables were on board. Turns out the pool tables weighed a ton and we did not expect the airplane to pay off on landing. Boy, we hit the runway...

"Fire truck, please!"

One of the duties of an instructor pilot supervisor at San Angelo was to man the runway control during student training periods. We always had a fire truck setting next to the control cab. One day an instructor called on the radio for a "fire truck, please". The fire engine wouldn't start, so the pilot taxied like hell toward us with the B-25, pouring smoke out of the rear compartment. Someone had left some old oily ropes in the airplane and they had started to smolder.

All students solo—Friday mornings

This activity was one where I was willing to beg for forgiveness rather than ask for permission first. I knew that I would never be given permission by our squadron to require all solo student activity to only be allowed on Fridays of the week we flew early mornings. But I would not allow any solo flying except on those days after the students had reached the solo stage. Then either the deputy flight commander or myself (flight commander) would come out and get them in the air. The instructors did not have to come out unless they were called, and then they had to be there in 30 minutes. No one at the Stage or Squadron level ever knew I did this, but the instructors sure liked it.

Opposite Flight Commander—"We know what we are doing"

We shared a flight shack with our opposite squadron flight. When we flew mornings, they flew afternoons and we traded off each week. My instructors were getting a little lax in having the students perform maneuvers such as stalls in various configurations and other air maneuvers, which were really fairly boring, although necessary. I put a list on the blackboard of each maneuver and how many of each had to be accomplished before soloing. When an instructor came to me and said his students were ready for solo, but lacked so many of this or that, I would make an assessment and if they were close, tell the instructor to let them go. These were in a sense my requirements to make sure we were covered. The other flight commander, not knowing where these requirements came from was holding all of his instructors to getting every one of the maneuvers. The students in that flight were grumbling that their counterparts were all soloing, and they were upset. I heard the other flight commander telling them one day that he knew the others were soloing, but he was going to stick to the requirement, and assured them that he knew what he was doing. Frank never had a clue as to what he was doing.

Stage Commander "Chew out" note

The Stage Commander was not able to reach anyone in the flight

I headed and so he traveled to the flight to find out that everyone was working, but not necessarily following standard operating procedures with all of the sign-out requirements. I always asked for more airplanes than I could man, because the squadron always cut my requests. This time maintenance came up with an airplane in the middle of the flying session and I had an outstanding request for more airplanes.

The following was a handwritten note on lined paper left for me by the Stage Commander:

Tues 25 Sept. 1500

> *Clawson:*
>
> *When you commit for 2 a/c for local, be damn sure you have someone here to fly them. Catlin called about 1330 and no one knew who was to fly the one a/c we gave you at 1300. 1400 to 1500 there wasn't anyone here to answer telephone to take 2nd a/c, and it had to be turned back. I came down about 1515—no one here, then Smith walked in—just returned from flt.*
>
> *Best you see me in am and put a stop to this crap. When supervisors leave everyone goes. I don't even know who is flying the one a/c—no schedule, no sign out, no nothing.*
>
> *Walker*

Clawson's too far ahead of Schedule

Every time a class got close to graduating it was necessary to give them extra airplanes and instructors to get them out on time. The classes always graduated on time, but what a hassle! I saw this when I was an element leader and determined that I would not run a flight this way. The Training Command put out a program for meeting the schedule. No one ever used it. I did, every class was programmed all the way to the end, and I intentionally fudged some of the airplane requests knowing that I would be cut back. Usually I got exactly what I needed to stay ahead of schedule. Even when I got too far ahead and they started cutting me back I had enough padded to stay ahead, and that used to drive the Stage Commander nuts. That is what contributed to the "Chew out" note above.

C-47 Crew Chief "liberating" 55-gallon drum of Isopropyl

We had flown a group of civilian mechanics from Goodfellow to Kelley AFB, in San Antonio, for some briefings. We were hit by lightning and one of the civilians wanted to jump. We had to restrain him for a minute. On the ground, the regular crew chief on this Base C-47 was tired of flying in icing conditions with no Isopropyl for de-icing the props, so he liberated a 55 gallon drum of the stuff and then borrowed a forklift to carry it to the airplane. As he approached the airplane he was hollering for us to open the door. He got it in and we had de-icing fluid for a while.

"Where did those Navy jets come from?"

I was flying the Base C-47 into Randolph Field, Texas and had just cleared the active when a Navy jet landed in the opposite direction to traffic. We asked the tower where the jet came from and why it was landing the wrong way. The tower said they had no radio contact with the jets. The first one to land ran off the end of the runway and had an accident. The next one landed and ran out of fuel and had to be towed to the ramp. The third one had crash-landed short of the runway. They had flown non-stop from San Diego and didn't have enough fuel.

Crew Chief took off his cap and threw it on the ground

John Newsom and I had just pulled our B-25s into his line after flight. We always had lots of write-ups. The Crew Chief recognized us and took his cap off and threw it on the ground and stomped on it. He knew he would be working late.

"You got thrown out of the Dipping Vat"?

Early on we had established a tradition of taking the departing instructors out for dinner and it usually ended up pretty raucous. One of our favorite haunts was a bar and restaurant out in the country, called the Dipping Vat. The Dipping Vat was not exactly a highbrow place and most anything went as far as raising hell. When we had one of the going away dinners and came back and told our friends that we had been thrown out of the Dipping Vat, they were in awe.

No more Low-Level Missions—B-25s

Our students were given the opportunity to fly the B-25 at 500' above the ground. Off course most of us went lower in order to scare the sheep and the trains. One IP came back with about a half a mile of barbed wire wrapped around the fuselage of the airplane. It was Class 26 (beyond repair) and we stopped flying low level.

Hit in the chest by a duck at 10,000 feet

A student who had been eliminated from flight training for fear of flying was hitch-hiking on a B-25 going from San Angelo to New York. He was sitting in the nose section, which has plexiglass all around, in the middle of the night, when a duck came crashing through the glass and smashed onto his chest. He of course was a nervous wreck after that.

Hillbilly Pilots—Levis and sport shirts

Air Force finances were so bad that we were unable to obtain flying suits and jackets and so we all wore Levis and sport shirts. When we would land at another base, the Crew Chiefs went nuts trying to figure out how we had gotten hold of this B-25. The question was always, "Where are the pilots?"

There's three people with parachutes hitch-hiking…

A B-25 lost an engine on take-off on a night student-training mission. The IP reached around the student pilot to pull the fuel shut-off valve, got the wrong one, and landed in a graveyard on downwind. I was also flying that night and a number of airplanes were hunting for them. We damn near ran into one another. Every chicken coop looked like a B-25. A car stopped at the main entrance to the base and told the Air Policeman that there was three people with parachutes on their backs hitch-hiking on the road south of the Base. They of course sent a vehicle for them right away to get them off the road.

ANG Base—Van Nuys, CA: Notam'd Out

When we went on cross-country flights and landed at other bases we were required to check Notices to Airmen (Notams) during mission planning for any outages of navigation facilities en-route or service limitations at the base of intended landing. Most of the time this was done routinely. One trip to Van Nuys was the exception. Van Nuys was a civilian field with an Air National Guard unit. The overlooked Notam advised that the unit was deployed for summer camp and there would be no government services, including fuel.

The weather was bad and we landed very shy on fuel. An emergency requisition would possibly be rejected and we'd be required to reimburse the Government. We called the fueling unit at Lockheed Air Terminal in Burbank, about ten miles away, and asked if they could bring us fuel. No, they couldn't, their contract was for delivering fuel at Lockheed. I said, "That's a shame, we would need about 950 gallons." The fellow said, "Where are you parked?", and they were right over. The receipt showed we were serviced at Lockheed and no one ever knew the difference.

Air Scout Clawson, T-O from Van Nuys

Another time at Van Nuys we were fueled and the ground crew also serviced the oil. It was necessary to go out the hatch above the cockpit to do this. Later that day I took my younger brother, who was an Air Scout, flying, which was legal. But, putting him in the left seat and letting him make the take-off was probably stretching it. On take-off, while I watching him closely, the hatch started to leave and I had the throttles to back up, and the hatch to hold on to, until I could get the other instructor who was with us to come forward and help me latch it. Again, no one ever knew.

ANG F-86 gear problem

Later that same day at Van Nuys, my brother and the other instructor were in the Base Ops and heard the tower call operations with word that an F-86, one of the ANG aircraft, could not get its gear down, was short on fuel, and wanted to know where ops wanted them to land the airplane. The Airman 3rd Class came right back with, "Wherever he can!"

An officer would probably still be trying to figure out where to land it…

"Ra Ra Time"—Squadron Officer School (SOS) Montgomery, Alabama

When I was selected to attend SOS I felt I was making progress in the Air Force. I soon found out that playing soccer, the den mother's choice, drinking beer afterwards, and planning parties constituted a major portion of the curriculum. One of my family members on active duty now had the same complaint. Because I chose to fly back to San Angelo one weekend rather that plan and attend a unit party, I was classed as "slightly above average for an officer of my grade". The rest of my professional education was completed by correspondence. Just to spite them, I think, I completed the Command and Staff Course, Air War College, and the Industrial College of the Armed Forces course "Emergency Management of the National Economy". While at the school we had many fine guest speakers. Major General Orvil Anderson, USAF, (Retired), spoke to us as described below.

"If I had the weapons and delivery means, we'd go tonight"

Major General Orvil Anderson, the first Commandant of the new US Air Force War College, spoke to a civic group in Montgomery, Alabama in 1950, advocating that the US give serious thought to bombing the Soviet Union with nuclear weapons. This was after North Korea had invaded South Korea with obvious help and encouragement from the Soviet Union.

This pre-emptive strike, or preventive war concept, was widespread in the Air Force. Since nuclear weapon expenditure is tightly held at the highest levels in the US and in most other nuclear capable countries, the discussion brought about Anderson's dismissal from the Air War College and his retirement at the end of the year.

The troubling part of this though is that even after five years, he was brought back to lecture classes in the Air University system. I attended the fall class in 1955 of the Squadron Officers' School, and he spent an hour or so lecturing on the evils of the Soviet Union and Communism. He made an unequivocal statement that if he had the weapons and the means of delivery, he would not wait until tomorrow to go, he would go tonight and bomb the Soviet Union.

(General Anderson was retired December 31, 1950 and died August 23, 1965. He established a world record ascent November 11, 1935 with the National Geographic /Army Air Corps Stratosphere balloon *Explorer II* of 72, 395 feet.)

The Air Force Training Command was very wise in restricting the tour of duty of the undergraduate flying school instructor to three years. It became very obvious that after watching the same mistakes over and over and interacting with these young fire-eaters that it was time for the instructor to move on after those three years. I applied for Navigator Training for Pilots at Waco, Texas, with a subsequent assignment to Davis-Monthan AFB in Tucson, and was granted both.

Chapter III: B-47 Operational Bomb Wing

Davis-Monthan AFB is located near Tucson, Arizona, with an elevation of over 3,000 feet above mean sea level. The runway was approximately 13,000 feet long oriented roughly north-west—south-east and far from level. It dipped in a couple of places and had a general upslope toward the north-west. The prevailing wind made the north-west runway the preferred runway. This also took the aircraft almost directly over the University of Arizona on departure. The Air Force storage and disposal organization was also located at the base.

The base was under the Strategic Air Command and 15th Air Force at March AFB, Riverside, California with its colorful Commander, Lieutenant General Archie Old. The base was very extensive with two bomber wings and one tanker squadron. Subordinate commanders at all levels tend to immolate the chiefs. General Old's favorite was to throw the telephone out the window when angered. Subordinate commanders throughout the 15th Air Force were known to pattern their behavior after his.

After completing the six-month course of Navigation Training for Pilots at James Connally AFN in Waco, Texas, I was assigned to the 43rd Bombardment Wing, at Davis Monthan AFB. When I arrived at Davis Monthan in July 1957 the 43rd Bomb Wing was deployed to Guam for normal rotation. Certain people remained at the base in Tucson and others were sent home for various reasons. I had been appointed one of the rear echelon squadron commanders.

Appointed Rear Echelon Squadron Commander

The Rear Echelon Wing Commander instructed the rear echelon squadron commanders, of which I was one, to paint all the barracks while the Wing was deployed to Guam. This was more to ingratiate himself with the returning Wing Commander than because of any real need. I started out to comply and quickly found out that there was no paint to be had for this purpose through supply channels. About this time, a new master sergeant was assigned to the squadron as the First Sergeant, and he said, "Just leave it to me." Sure enough, pretty soon he came down the street with enough paint in the back of his car to paint half the base. He had traded our beds for the paint with one of the supply personnel.

Don't worry about the aircrews

When the Wing was redeploying from Guam, a lot of anxiety was expressed about taking care of the ground crews and notifying families when to expect them and other nice things to do. Someone brought up the fact that no notices were being given the aircrews' families, and the answer came back that the aircrews took care of themselves and their families had better information than the wing.

Top Secret Document Inventory

Because I arrived at Davis Monthan without B-47 training I was given all sorts of trivial jobs. One of them was to do the six-month inventory of all Top Secret Documents in the Wing. In order to count the documents present the inventory officer had to sight the document. The certification I was required to sign upon completion said that if I found Top Secret material that was not properly controlled, I should take immediate steps to bring it under control. When I went to the War Plans shop I found rooms full of Top Secret material, uncontrolled. I went back to the Major who was the Wing Executive Officer, and told him I could not sign the statement because I had been thrown out of War Plans when I told them they had to control all of the working material that was stamped Top Secret. He took the certification and changed it so I could sign it.

We had another problem when I could not locate twenty some cases of Top Secret war plans material that was signed for by an officer in the Tanker Squadron. That officer had been reassigned over a year before. The Tanker Squadron Commander, nicknamed "Big Bear", became very hostile when I kept coming back insisting that they had the documents. Finally, I went through this huge building that was a "blockhouse" with a safe door for an entrance, and found many documents that were supposed to have been destroyed, and the missing twenty some cases of a war plan used by the Tanker Squadron at Dyess AFB when they took over the war plan for the 43rd Tanker Squadron. The Executive Officer half heartily thank me for doing the inventory, and added that I would never be asked to do it again.

Shot down on first burst

Again, looking for something for me to do, the squadron scheduler sent me to the firing range at Tucson where B-47 tail guns were set up on the ground to train co-pilots. The guns were radar controlled, and live target drones were flown toward the guns. I set up and locked on the first drone, and fired a burst; it hit the engine and destroyed it, breaking the propeller when it hit the ground. The Sergeant who was acting as my instructor asked if I wanted the prop; it still hangs in my den. He also typed up a certification that I knocked down the target with the first burst.

Boneyard Commander—Flying B-47

Because the Storage Yard commander, an old full Colonel, lived near me in Tucson he would drive into my driveway and honk his horn. I would have to go out and talk to him for a while. He had watched while we had built our own home and he frequently stopped while we were working on it. Later he had orders to put some airplanes in flying condition from his inventory of B-47s to be used as drone targets. He had one flying when the order came to cease the operation. No order was given to place the flyable 47 back in storage, so he went to a bomb squadron at Davis Monthan and talked an IP into flying with him and they used to fly that airplane all over the place.

Stead AFB- Advanced Survival School SAC

January 1958 was the middle of one cold winter, especially when you are expected to live in a simulated prison camp for a few days and nights being interrogated and starved. When we got out of that we were taken directly west of Stead, into the Sierra Nevadas in California and told, "You and your seven team members are to have one live rabbit, a few potatoes, one onion and some

Fig.12 B-52G with Hound Dog air-to-surface missiles

pemmican to eat for eight days".

The skinny guys had a hell of a time. The pemmican was so terrible, I gave mine to the scrawny ones. Normally the last night of the trek was an escape and evasion exercise, but it was snowing so hard and they had lost a couple of officers in the class before for several days, so the instructors had to stay with us. With parkas drawn up around our heads, and the snow so heavy, we looked like the Germans retreating from Moscow. We were so soaked that a number of the students dug down to mineral soil, started a big bonfire, and removed all their clothes to try an dry them out. That was a sight—25 or 30 big guys, in the middle of the night, naked with snow everywhere, trying to dry their clothes out!

After waiting for several months for a training slot, I was sent to various training bases to transition into the B-47. When the unit returned from Guam, the squadron operations officer said that they had enough pilots and they intended to send me to school to upgrade as a navigator. This I rejected totally and then he thought it would be a good idea if I flew in the back seat as a co-pilot for a while, to which I replied that I was qualified for the front seat (Aircraft Commander) and that was what I expected. He then said, "Okay."

Project Milk Bottle Crack—McConnell AFB

Our IP wanted to go see a B-47 with a crack in the wing large enough to put your whole hand in. I declined and so did the student co-pilot, who had already been in a major B-47 accident at Homestead AFB. SAC had disconnected Fire Warning Lines on their aircraft, but Training Command had not. That day we had two actual engine fires, but kept on shooting touch and gos. The IP was worried that the Tower Officer might detect that there was no exhaust coming from those engines and make us stop.

In my spare time I bought a nice lot out toward Mount Lemon in a beautiful subdivision and proceeded to build an adobe house. One of the things about building a house that I did not like to do was paint. Therefore when I could afford it I hired painters. One of them was a local fireman who did this on his time off. He was okay painting the outside and under the roof on the overhang and the carport. We ask him if he did wallpapering—answer, yes. He spent all of one day working in a small portion of the bathroom trying to hang the paper and all he accomplished was that he ruined the expensive wallpaper my wife had bought. He agreed to pay for the paper he ruined but he wanted to be paid for the time it took him to ruin it. I told him to pound sand.

You have to pay your bills

I received a call from a self-appointed executive officer of my squadron at Davis Monthan one night telling me in a high-pitched voice that this man had called the base and wanted to get them to make me pay him. I told the so called executive officer that it was none of his business, never to call me with this sort of thing again, and told him if he wanted to call the guy back, tell him to sue me. I never heard anything about it again. This sort of thing used to make me mad because locals thought that if they called the base over a disagreement with an Air Force member that the Air Force was obligated to coerce the member into paying. Many times it was over things just such as this.

As I was going out the gate at Davis Monthan on my way to Little Rock, I heard the base siren and knew that some sort of an alert had been called. Since my job was to go to Little Rock to become Combat Ready, I knew I was not needed at the squadron so I kept on going. When I arrived at Little Rock, the unit I was to train with had deployed. All of the instructors were aircraft commanders (a/c) so when a co-pilot reported for upgrading to a/c they put him in the back seat and launched another B-47 to an overseas base. They had a weather reconnaissance mission and so went all over the world. We had to wait until the airplanes and instructors returned to start our training.

Pull up! We're going to collide—TDY Little Rock AFB

The co-pilot assigned to my crew was a pretty fair pilot, but scared all the time. During training at Little Rock AFB, we had several solo missions where we flew navigation missions and once landed at Tampa, Florida. Going into Tampa, approach control called out traffic at 10 o'clock traveling south. I saw the other aircraft and he was well below us and clear of our track. The co-pilot latched onto a ground light and screamed over the interphone for me to pull up as we were going to collide with it. I didn't pay any attention to his call and proceeded with the penetration and approach and landing. He took great exception to this when we got on the ground, and said I didn't have any faith in him. I didn't.

On the way back to Little Rock the next night we were flying in clear weather toward the west and I noticed Polaris as being very clear and bright. Because the B-47 had a noticeable "Dutch Roll" (roll around the longitudinal axis of the airplane) when on autopilot, it appeared that the star Polaris was moving. Again, I was slightly dozing when I hear this scream over the interphone to alter course, we were about to collide with something. This guy was a Nervous Nelly.

Little Rock AFB APs playing Quick Draw

During the Lebanon Crisis (1958) the base at Little Rock, like all SAC Bases, was on a heightened state of alert. The APs on guard at a little used gate were bored and decided to see who could draw the fastest. In the act of playing, one shot the other in the foot. The Provost Marshal took all the bullets away from all of the MPs.

Loose Bomb at Little Rock AFB

When the Lebanon Crisis subsided it was necessary to download the bombs on the generated sorties and return them to the nuclear weapons Storage Area. The crews handling Nuclear Weapons are pretty sharp, but they also had a sense that they knew when weapons were safely in the bomb bay and used to scare the hell out of me with dropping the rack once they heard certain clicks. Unloading the weapons must have been second nature to them, but, they dropped one on the ramp and caused a Broken Arrow (incident involving Nuclear Weapons) to be declared.

Low Clouds and Visibility-Holding and Watching Crash Site

We were TDY for training at Little Rock AFB. One morning we had to hold for prolonged period due to missing aircraft in the area from Fort Worth. There had been a crash the night before just to the left of the runway, and five crew-members had been killed. We watched emergency vehicles for an hour or so which did not enhance our desire to fly that day. After and hour or so, our training mission was cancelled and we returned to the ramp. I was just as glad.

Boy, riding that motorcycle is just too dangerous!

One day we had completed our preflight on the B-47 we were to fly around in all night and we were on the ramp under the nose of the airplane and the navigator was relating how one of our friends had a motorcycle and how dangerous it was, especially since he had little children. The co-pilot responded, "What the hell do you think flying this thing [pointing to the B-47], with Clawson is—a walk in the park?"

STRATEGIC AIR COMMAND MANAGEMENT CONTROL SYSTEM (MCS)

Once we finished combat crew training, survival training and were given briefings on our Emergency War Order (EWO), we were fully subject to the MCS. This really meant that we had to learn to be successful on each and every mission regardless of what it required. The Management Control System (MCS) was devised to grade each activity the SAC wing engaged in. This made it possible to compare results of each wing in SAC and determine who was best and who needed help. It also provided the opportunity for each Wing Commander to show his ingenuity.

The navigators really had the hardest job in this respect. They had to be extremely proficient in backing in each type of navigation leg flown. A day grid navigation leg was difficult enough, but it also had to be reliable. This type of navigation was used in the extreme northern latitudes due to unreliable compass readings. A day grid mission was made all the more difficult since there was only the sun for celestial observations.

Consider that the overall average circular error probable (CEP) for all types of navigation legs flown during a full training quarter in the 43rd Bomb Wing was 1.5 miles, and you can see how efficient the navigators had become in backing in the legs flown. The 15th Air Force Inspector General (IG) sent a team of staff navigators to investigate how we did so well. Now these guys were some of the best cheaters in SAC, that's the way they were selected for their jobs. They could not find any discrepancies in the documentation of the missions. We also over flew targets assigned in the Radar Bomb Scoring System (RBS) to measure our precise altitude before going out to the pre-initial point (PIP) to commence the bomb run. The term for getting ahead in SAC was lie, cheat and steal. It was a real kick in the pants to learn that the Soviets had adopted the same system for the Soviet Rocket Forces and the Air Defense Forces. They really were able to make their units look good. They had been doing this very same kind of swindle with their ground forces and civilian industry reporting for decades.

After completing the training in Arkansas we returned to upgrade to combat ready status and start developing our skills at beating the Management Control System (MCS), which was truly the name of the game. The navigators took longer learning how to back in Navigation training legs than being competent at doing it the legal way, but backing in a Nav leg while on final approach to land was the real test. Backing in a navigation leg involved concocting celestial observations and other fix points in such a way as to be able to plot them and come out with a destination point that was within the criteria of being "reliable".

My crew went on to be the best B-47 crew in the 43rd Bomb Wing for the quarter of May-August 1959. By the time we were presented our plaques, by the Wing Commander testifying to our competence, we were in the cellar. The Nav had thrown several bad bombs and screwed up a Nav leg and so we got to start all over making a name for ourselves.

A crew that had a navigator that could consistently drop good Radar Bombing Scoring (RBS) bombs, and was competent in backing in Navigation legs had the key to spot promotions. Once in a while if I came down too hard on my navigator, he would just look at me and say he owed me a bad bomb, which would get us a trip to the "barbecue" (critique in the Wing Command Post) the next day, where I would take most of the heat.

One training quarter when our wing was neck and neck with the 303rd Bomb Wing, also located on Davis Monthan, an airman went absent without official leave (AWOL). No one could find him and it was a sure thing that if he was reported on the morning report as AWOL, the wing would automatically be out of the running for the best wing in all of SAC. The Wing Commander briefed the entire wing on the circumstances and made it abundantly clear that no one was to discuss the matter outside that room. If the 303rd heard about it, they were going to be declared the winner. No one talked; the Wing Commander said that when the airman was found, he might do him in.

"You do, and I'll tell Clawson—he'll wrap a fire extinguisher round your head!"

As I have explained the co-pilot assigned to my crew was a pretty fair pilot, but scared all the time. He did okay until we were briefed on our EWO. Then he really came unglued. He told the Navigator that he didn't want to fly one night and was going to wait until we were going fast enough on the take-off, to where we would have to deploy the brake chute to abort, and then call an abort. The Nav told him that if he did that he would tell Clawson and "he'll wrap a fire extinguisher around your head". He didn't try it. He was so bad from then on Lt. Colonel Richard Dunlap, our squadron commander, obtained a discharge for him. He later joined the Tucson Police Department, went through training with flying colors, and the first time he got shot at, quit.

Crews and Equipment

The crews worked very hard to achieve the best results possible with the equipment we had. The B-47 and KC-97 (developed from the B-29) were totally incompatible. The refuelings were almost worthless as far as adding range to the B-47. The KC-97 could not fly fast enough to give us a good platform to refuel from, it was required that we be in a descent and the tanker had to use Maximum Except Take-off (METO) power to go fast enough to keep the bomber from stalling as we took on the additional weight of the fuel. Accidents and incidents were infrequent, but what was sometimes scary is shown by the next anecdote. Cheating was not unknown of but not spoken of except when we were in a bind and needed to catch up on the MCS points.

B-47 through KC-97 props on Night Refueling Mission

Joe Pavlas was a student at Navigation School at Waco with me. He told some of the most hair-raising stories about flying the KC-97 that we had heard. Most of us dismissed them as "War Stories" that were probably exaggerated. Then he flew a B-47 through the props of a KC-97 on a night refueling mission and tore the hell out of the tail. Maintenance parked it right outside our Squadron building for the whole world to see "Pavlas's Folly". While en route to Tucson from Waco, Joe and his wife, Mary, left a cat at a roadside rest stop and didn't realize it for 200 miles. They turned around and retrieved the cat. They were always misplacing one of their kids.

While The 303rd Bomb Wing was also stationed at Davis Monthan, traditionally the two wings, the 43rd and the 303rd, were first and second among he B-47 wings in SAC as far as MCS points were concerned. A great deal of competitive spirit existed. Secrecy regarding breaches of regulations was almost completely successful. An example of this occurred when the airman from the 43rd went AWOL one quarter and this was briefed to the 43rd Wing Officers but never reported on the daily reports to higher headquarters because it would cause the wing to lose out in the

The Commanders of the subordinate units in the Wing were very conscious of the necessity to maximize the MCS points available. Knowing that the only way the Wing Commander was going to make General was to be on top and that their performance reports depended on the maximum effort of their subordinates they sometimes lost their cool.

Squadron Commander Throwing Clothes on Floor

The 43rd B. W. was in contention for the best B-47 wing in SAC, and our squadron had just one sortie still in the air at the end of the quarter. All they had to do was make reliable bomb runs and Navigation legs and we would win. This did not mean that the runs had to be anything special, just within the reliability range. The Squadron Commander met the airplane crew when they landed, only to find out that they had an unreliable bomb run. He was so upset that he left immediately went home and had a fit. One of the squadron staff felt compelled to go to his house to see if he was okay. He found that he had taken all of his clothes out of the closets and thrown them all over the floor. He did go on to become a full colonel at 15th Air Force Headquarters.

B-47 Refueling—KC-97's Shut-off Valve stuck open

We were refueling at night with a KC-97 east of Phoenix, Arizona, which was over a mountainous region. The KC-97 could not go fast enough for us without descending while we were hooked up. In the early stages I needed more time than others to learn to refuel so this night I had worked pretty hard at it and when we were finally finished we disconnected, but the shut-off valve in the boom stuck open. The tanker pilot wanted me to reconnect to shut the valve off. This meant driving up behind this floating gas station with fuel pouring out and connect. That was dicey because the static electricity that builds up on airplanes could present a hazard with all that fuel pouring all over the airplane. It worked, though, and no damage was done.

B-47 attempts refueling with KC-97 playing games

Another day we were refueling with a KC–97 from the 43rd

Bomb Wing that was to meet us for refueling in about the same area as the above incident. We were right on our speed schedule for the distance being called out by the navigator, and suddenly I realized we were going to pass this guy like a freight train. I asked him what his speed was and he laughed and said it was about 100 knots too low for a schedule. We had to make a big circle and come in behind him again; this time we were successful. I gave him a piece of my mind and we left.

Squadron Commander: "Don't you ever lie to me!"

One day the Squadron Commander was questioning me about an activity I had taken a part in. It was not exactly according to SAC regulations and he admonished me not to tell him such things, just do what was necessary. The activity had to do with cheating on bomb runs by overflying the target area and having the navigator measure the *precise* altitude and then going out to the pre-initial point (Pre-IP) and calling the radar bomb site for a simulated bomb run. We had been instructed to do this by the Bomb-Nav section at the wing level. I told him that I was getting confused as to when I was to lie to him and when to tell him the truth. He roared at me, "Don't you ever lie to me!"

> The competition was so severe between Wings that the Wing Commanders (WC) used rather bizarre management techniques to get people to do their best. One such technique was to hold a meeting in the command post following every training day. This was know as the "stand-up briefing", because no one sat down. It was better know as the "barbecue". During one such briefing the Wing Commander related what went wrong with the mission he had flown the day before.
>
> The mission had gone as planned until upon arriving in the local area and near traffic pattern altitude, the WC called for the drag chute to be deployed. This chute was used when the weight of the B-47 was such that to fly final approach and stay on the speed schedule the pilot would have to retard the throttle to full idle without the chute. Since the J-47 engine was notorious for taking a long time to spool up to produce thrust it was dangerous in the event of an event requiring immediate thrust. This chute provided enough drag that the throttles had to be fairly far forward. The chute had a maximum speed of 195 knots. The airspeed indicator had two hands like a clock, one for hundreds and one for tenths. The WC was actually traveling at near 280 knots when he instructed the co-pilot to

deploy the chute, and the pin holding the chute to the airplane did just what it was supposed to do—it failed, and the chute went into the desert.

What the hell did you think you were back there for?

The co-pilot was actually an instructor pilot (IP), who was required each time the Wing Commander (WC) flew a mission. It was his primary job to keep the old man out of trouble. As the crew approached the base for landing it was necessary because of their weight to deploy an approach chute to allow the pilot to keep the throttles forward to keep the spool-up time as low as possible in the event of a go around on final approach. He didn't fly that often, so he was not quite as sharp at the controls as most of the line pilots. The WC misread the airspeed indicator, which had a vernier scale, which read out first the 100s, and then the hundredths. The WC raised hell with the IP for not correcting the mistake before deploying the chute because the airspeed was just a hundred miles too fast… The chute failed as predicted but the WC wasn't taking any of the blame for the loss of the chute and made it clear that he had a very low opinion of the IP that day.

"You cost us the only abort in May"

My crew and I were on leave for the first time since upgrading to the B-47 and had not flown in several weeks. We were due back on Monday for mission planning to fly on Tuesday night. The Friday before I received a call to come out to the base because there had been a late take-off that morning due to engine trouble on a B-47, and they needed to at least fly it around the traffic pattern to avoid losing MCS points due to a cancellation. The late take-off didn't cost as many points. The maintenance people assured us they had corrected the problem, and loaded the aircraft with minimum fuel so that we could turn downwind and land immediately after take-off.

We took the runway, feeling a little less than confident about the whole operation, added full throttle, released the brakes and started rolling; not long after, all the engine instruments on one engine, the same one that had caused the morning aborted take-off—began spinning erratically, so we pulled the throttles to idle and deployed the brake chute. It was almost four in the afternoon and the wing commander had established that 4P.M. on Fridays was the deadline for any take-offs. We were later accused by several crew-members and staff of having *caused* the only abort in May for the entire Wing.

In February 1959 SAC had levied a requirement for a task force of B-47s to deploy to Elmendorf AFB, Alaska, for the purpose of flying high and low altitude missions against the radars on the Aleutian Islands. Several interesting incidents took place due to this deployment. Our Squadron Commander was the task force commander for this exercise. The crews came from other squadrons at Davis Monthan as well as those from our squadron.

B-47 Crew "Mayday" over Northwest Territories

Several B-47s from Davis Monthan were instructed to proceed to Elmendorf AFB, in a simulated bomber stream. The aircrews were to perform an abbreviated training mission en route. Normally on a Navigation leg, the radar is supposed to be detuned so that it can't be used to check on the progress of the mission. That's what the crew ahead of us did, and upon approaching Skagway we heard, "Mayday, mayday!" We called the crew and told them to turn on their radar beacon and our navigator found them heading north in the Northwest Territories in Canada and gave them a new heading to Elmendorf. Of course this had them entering the Air Defense Identification Zone (ADIZ) in the wrong place, so they got a violation for that.

They caught hell when they landed and were then scheduled for one of the operational missions we were flying. Shortly after take-off they called the command post saying that their radar was inoperative and would be aborting the mission and returning to Elmendorf. When they landed, maintenance found that the crew had flown with the radar controls in dummy load. The dummy load position on the radar set allows the crew to run the radar without actually emitting a signal, but does nothing for navigation or bombing. The task force commander kicked a drawer in the old wooden desk in his office clear out the other side.

The crew was grounded. Spent time refueling B-47s—in -50° weather—waiting for a KC 97 coming from Davis Monthan with a Standardization Crew on board, to give a no-notice Stand Board flight to the crew back to Tucson on their B-47. Amazingly, the purpose of the Stand Board check was to upgrade the crew to Senior Status so they were eligible for the quota the Wing had for a "plum" B-52 assignment.

Honest, General, I won't ever do that again

One of the aircraft commanders was a Southern boy and always had a rebel flag sticking out of the cockpit when he taxied to and from the runway and during pre-flight. In Alaska we never opened the canopy so he had to stick it in the snow in front of the airplane. He had a very distinct accent so you always knew who was talking over the radio. This got him into trouble with the other Wing Commander one night. While we were flying these missions in Alaska we were suppose to cooperate with the Air Defense Command. The F-102 fighters would bounce us going and coming and the rules of engagement said the bomber was to take no evasive action or other kinds of quick maneuvers while under "attack".

Even though we were not going too fast, the F-102 had to attack at 1.1 mach and still ended in a tail chase. This guy would wait until they were committed at a 90 degree angle to us and then roll his airplane up into a 60 degree bank and turn right into them, scattering them all over the place. Of course they reported this and the General gave him hell at the next briefing. He actually raised his right hand and swore that he would not repeat this. The next mission he did the exact same thing. I guess he just couldn't "hep" himself.

This was the same guy who always hoisted a rebel flag out the hatch after landing a B-47 anywhere. He could not do this at Fairbanks, because we never opened the hatch. So he took to planting the flag in the snow in front of the airplane while he was doing the pre-flight.

National Guard doesn't fly on Sundays

On one of our last missions out of Fairbanks, Alaska took us out the Aleutian Chain and back over land towards the base. No fighters had been up this day and we queried the GCI site. He said the regulars were standing down today, and the only aircraft was an Air National Guard F-89 at Ladd AFB, but they had not intended to scramble him. The guys gave them such a bad time about the National Guard not flying on Sunday that they launched him. We saw him coming up, but he could not get to our altitude until we were way past him, so we had to go without an attack that day.

"Chief, You Have to Check the Forward Aux Tank"—Alaska

On most deployments the crew stays with the aircraft that they deployed with. This was done in Alaska. When we left Davis Monthan the forward auxiliary fuel tank gauge resembled the old Model T Ford fuel gauge. It was either full, empty or intermediate. The gauge was obviously malfunctioning when we left but it was either intermediate or full. We had other trouble with the forward aux tank and the crew chief had to empty it and replace a pump. He worked all night doing it in very low temperatures so that the airplane would be mission ready in the morning. Since the forward auxiliary fuel tank was very critical with regard to the balance of the airplane and dictated where the trim was set for take-off, the procedure during pre-flight was that the flight crew always opened the tank and checked it visually to see that it was full. This morning the ground crew was de-icing the aircraft and goop was flowing all down the sides. I did not open the tank and check it visually. When we were ready to start engines, I saw out of my peripheral vision that the tank had flashed empty on the gauge. I called to the crew chief to check it and he was very chagrined to tell us that it was empty. We had an abort. We couldn't get fuel fast enough to make the mission, so a back-up flew.

We had been told that if the trim were set for a full tank, and a take-off was attempted with an empty aux tank, there was no way you could control the airplane as it went over the top of a loop on take-off.

If you can't go on time, we'll just cancel the mission"—Alaska

The runways were very treacherous due to thick ice. The procedure used by the crews for take-off included setting the brakes and running the throttles full open and stabilizing the engines before releasing them. This took several seconds and there was always a countdown by the Navigator to release brakes. This was tried at Elmendorf, but the airplane would be sliding down the runway with the brakes set, so the crews would release and keep going. In debriefing, the General Officer critiquing the mission that rolled 20 seconds early made the statement that if we couldn't go on time, we would just scrub the missions. Everyone rolled their eyes on that one.

> *There had been too many instances where the brake chute was not installed properly for use on landing, so it became standard operating procedure for the aircraft commander to hook up the chute and stow it on the pre-flight. I had done that at Davis Monthan before departing for Fairbanks, Alaska.*

"No brake chute—watch out!"

On landing at Elmendorf AFB, Fairbanks, Alaska there was snow and ice over the entire base. We pulled the handle to deploy the brake chute, which we could really have used here; nothing happened. The "follow me" truck that met us when we left the runway on the high-speed turn-off really worked hard to keep ahead of us. Scared the hell out of him. Upon examination, the mechanism that accomplished the deployment of the chute when the handle was pulled after landing was broken.

"This guy will fly anything"

As a result of our TDY to Alaska in February, 1959, Lt. Col. Dickie Dunlap knew me a little better, and in the next ER. He wrote that "this officer is mission oriented, and can determine the difference between a safety of flight deficiency and a simple Dash One discrepancy." (The manual for the airplane, called the *Dash One*, covers all discrepancies, many of which do not involve safety of flight issues, and corrections are routinely delayed). I asked him not to say that again, because it looked to me that it said, "This guy will fly anything".

> *Because there were very few civilian airplanes flying above 25,000 feet, air traffic control systems had lagged behind what we were doing. There were no assigned altitudes for us to fly. We were supposed to fly at altitudes that corresponded to our course. That didn't always work, though, and such things as the next anecdote occurred.*

Flying Safety Bulletin: *B-47's Head-on Collision-Minor Damage*

I saw this headline on a flying safety bulletin in the squadron and couldn't believe it. After reading it I could easily relate to what had happened. Two B-47s were flying toward each other, which shouldn't have happened. Someone was not on the correct altitude, but with the rate of closure over 1,000 mph they did not see each other. Suddenly the top airplane lost three engines on the starboard side. That was the extent of the indications of trouble. They returned to base and found that the tail of another airplane had miraculously severed the fuel lines in the right wing, inboard of the number 4 engine, shutting down the number 4, 5 and 6 engines. SAC went out to all wings and instructed them to search for an airplane with appropriate damage. Shortly thereafter, a B-47 was found with a much-shortened tail.

> *At times the rules for flying a mission were so inflexible that the crews were unnecessarily endangered. The problem of flexibility was that the Wing Staff was full of innovative thinkers and would have always provided a rationale for change to accommodate the problem at hand. The lack of accommodation for a jump in the day's temperature, however, did put the crews in jeopardy and we would roll almost to the other end of the runway.*

Predicted temperature bust for Take-off Time

During summers in Tucson, the B-47s were loaded with fuel based on a predicted temperature at time of take-off. At times these predictions were significantly wrong and it put the crews in jeopardy. We would not be given an opportunity to start engines early to burn off the excess and so we just flew overweight for take-off calculations. At times because of the rolling nature of the runway you would see the airspeed indicator actually stop increasing or slightly decrease as you were rolling down the runway. More than once I could clearly see the "V's" at the far end of the runway. The overrun at each end of the runway have yellow "V's" painted on them pointing to the end of the actual runway. It would do no good to pull it off before time because you would simply lengthen the eventual roll. This was traditionally called "Pucker time".

Sometimes something like the following story would make you laugh and almost cry at the same time. The response we got from the controller was at the time hilarious, but in retrospect it was obvious that she had conflicting traffic and there could have been a catastrophe as a result of her delaying the instruction until it was not possible for us to comply.

Lady Approach Controller: "Oh, never mind"

We were inbound to the high station for a penetration to Davis Monthan. Departing high station with gear down and a rate of descent of 4,000' per minute we started a left penetration turn at one three thousand feet, and called approach control when we started our turn. The standard approach called for leveling at one zero thousand until inbound on final approach. The lady controller's response upon receiving our call was for us to level at one one thousand. We told her were already level at one zero thousand. Her response was an exasperated, "Oh, never mind!"

Several B-47 Wings supported the Alert Line at Anderson AFB, Guam, with airplanes and ground and air crews. The rotation was about every 45 days. Some crews had made the trip a number of times over the past several years. About four crews slept in trailers almost next to the airplanes to provide quick response to any alert. The balance came from quarters further away. Each crew was assigned a station wagon, and when an alert was sounded, all traffic left the roads to allow the alert crews priority.

"That's my number—TDY Guam

Through arrangements with communications, crews could call back to their home bases and the base would "patch" them through to their residences to talk to their families. The trailer crews could monitor conversations back to the States on the HF radio installed in the trailers. This made possible to know when a call was being completed and they could dial the last number necessary to contact the base communications office. One day we were monitoring calls in one of the trailers and someone made a call to March AFB switch and the caller asked for a number—it was the home of one of the guys who was listening with us in the trailer. He got to listen to the caller talking to his wife.

Overlap of Crews—TDY Guam

Since there were many civil service employees on Anderson AFB, many of whom were female, arrangements developed between them and some crew-members. There was normally no overlap of crews because the outgoing crews left on the airplane that brought the new crews inbound. Once in a while, though, the weather didn't cooperate and then there was an overlap and some very artful ducking and dodging.

Pinball Sign at Alert Gate—TDY Guam

To give the crews a heads up as to what kind of alert they were responding to, someone came up with the bright idea of putting what looked like a pin ball machine at the security gate going on the alert ramp which lit up the words describing the type of alert the crews were responding to. The problem one day was that some one in the command post pushed the wrong button and lit the "STRIKE" sign. This would have only been used in the event the crews were to strike their targets. It also meant that there would probably be incoming ICBMs to strike Anderson AFB on Guam. It was said that the aircrews couldn't get the ground crews out of the airplanes, they wanted to go with the bombers.

Rollover Danger at Alert Gate—Guam

The flight crews received complaints from the staff that they were taking the turn onto the alert ramp too fast, endangering the security personnel at the gate. The crews responded that the safest thing to do was put the security personnel on the other side of the driveway. Real no-brainer.

Night Alerts on Guam—produced more bodies from Rejects' Barracks than Crew Barracks

The special arrangements mentioned above with the civil service ladies included sleepovers at times. As a result, an alert in the middle of the night sometimes produced a large number of bodies coming out of the civilian barracks.

"Ban the Bomb" written on Mark 92 in Bomb Bay

Alert aircraft were under 24-hour guard and yet someone got in the bomb bay of one B-47 and wrote "Ban the Bomb" on it. This caused a Broken Arrow to be declared.

Smoke if you have them...

Upon approaching a B-47 on the alert line that was assigned to my crew I found the military policeman guarding it from under the nose of the aircraft, smoking a cigarette. What balls.

"This will be a random approach"—Yokota, Japan

Due to a typhoon approaching Guam, the alert line was dismantled and sent to Yokota, Japan. We weren't allowed to take nuclear weapons to Japan, so our aircraft was one of the last to leave Guam. When we arrived the Japanese controllers were less than happy to have a whole bomber stream coming into their system. They happily handed us off to the GI controllers who made you feel like they had you in their hand and were going to take care of you. My approach controller (GCA) came on the air saying that this would be a random approach. I never reached a heading he gave me that he hadn't already issued another, truly random, and we ended up right at the end of the runway.

Crew Briefing before Landing: No brake chute

Once we got to the Bachelor Officers' Quarters (BOQ) we were tired and near the Officers' Club. The really good booze was so cheap that I think we all tried to use it all up. At about four in the morning a staff officer woke us all to tell us we were going back to Guam at 0900 in the morning. My airplane had fuel gauge problems and I objected to flying it that way because of center of gravity problems. I was overruled and flew back with the bomber stream. A fuel selection made on the large fuel panel was not accomplished and the selector switch did not seat properly and so when the crew woke up over Iwo Jima, one engine was shut down. Several air starts did not work so we proceeded to Guam. There was a hefty crosswind and I instructed the co-pilot that we would not deploy the brake chute because of the danger of weathervaning, exaggerated by the one engine out. Soon after we landed the tower personnel at Anderson AFB called to say we had no chute. The co-pilot called out that he would get it and deployed it. I immediately jettisoned it and we rolled out on the runway with no problems.

We soon got into a routine of flying training missions that involved Mission Planning in the morning, which was completed by 11A.M., at which time the squadron staff would just as soon have the crews leave with the flight to take-off near midnight the next day, fly most or all that night and have the rest of the day off. In the next day or so the cycle started all over. Many incidents occurred during these training missions. Some are described below.

"This may sound weird, but try it"—Wing Commander

On one of our early combat training missions we were to participate in a higher headquarters directed mission that involved a refueling, bomb runs and Navigation training legs. The take-off and refueling produced the most MCS points, aborting the other items didn't cost too much. On take-off we could not retract all of the gear. The circuit-breaker, next to the co-pilot, for one gear kept popping. We called the command post and soon the Wing Commander was on the horn. He said we should follow his instructions even though it sounded weird, hold the circuit breaker in and retract the handle on the gear. Sure enough it worked and we headed for the refueling. As soon as we completed the refueling the tanker said to contact Oakland Center that they had message for us.

The Center relayed our command post's instruction to return to the Tucson area and *attempt* to get our gear down. We did, the gear came down and we landed as soon as the aircraft weight was low enough to get down.

Get your chute, chief, you're going with us

In doing our exterior inspection of the B-47 we were assigned, we found fuel around and in the battery compartment. This was discussed with the Crew Chief, who was under a great deal of pressure from his superiors to get the airplane off on time. It did not seem to bother him that there was an apparent leak near the compartment. He claimed that it was okay. We merely told him to get his chute, he was going with us—and he went directly to the maintenance vehicle and called for assistance in finding the source of the fuel and had it corrected. This is the only time I did this, but in this instance it worked. The discrepancy should have been fixed and rather than fight with him about it, telling him to go with us made the problem more personal.

"Supervisor of flying used poor judgment"

Another higher headquarters directed mission in which a number of aircraft from both wings were taking part was an all-night affair, flying all over the West Coast from Seattle to Los Angeles. As we taxied out it became very apparent that the N-1 compass system had failed since the compass needle kept doing 360s. We called for maintenance and a young airman came on board at the end of the runway and started kicking the hell out of the bulkhead under the co-pilot's feet. We threw him off the airplane and called that we were taxiing back to the ramp. The Supervisor of Flying (SOF) called from the command post and told us to go and stay VFR. We declined his suggestion. The next day I told our squadron operations officer that I thought the SOF had exercised damned poor judgment giving us that kind of advice. He said he was the SOF and expected me to follow instructions in the future. The N-1 compass system drove all the systems for navigation and bombing in the airplane.

Nobody but a dumb SAC pilot would be out here—we're safe

For some reason I flew a number of missions with our squadron operations officer and I never felt real smart in doing so. We took off for a low-level mission near Tucson and to the north-east of the base. This is a very mountainous area. The weather was bad and at times obscured the mountains. I was ill at ease and really thought we were foolish. He said we were safe, because nobody but a dumb SAC pilot would be out in this stuff.

> When we were on alert with nuclear weapons there was a strap-on harness around the fuselage just forward of the vertical stabilizer that held 30 bottles of ATO. These were, in effect, rockets and would provide a tremendous boost for heavyweight take-off. The ATO was fired by the pilot when the aircraft reached approximately 125 knots on take-off roll. There was a red guarded switch attached to the side of the number one throttle. As take-off was initiated, the guarded switch was exposed. The crews that were currently in the force had never taken off using ATO because of so many accidents. Supposedly they had fixed the problem and every aircraft commander was to make one 30-bottle ATO in the training quarter.

Fig.13   'Tall Tail' B-52 refueling from KC-135

Loss of shimmy dampener on right gear—ABORT

My turn to experience the 30-bottle trip came up and I was assigned a Wing staff member, Major Don Lamoine, to fly as co-pilot. I thought he was an instructor, but it turned out he was only co-pilot qualified at the time. We started our take-off roll, I uncapped the red guarded switch and we were headed for 125 knots. About 120 kt the throttles were yanked out of my hand and the chute deployed and we were aborting. I remember being mad as hell at first because of all the hell I had gotten for an earlier abort. But Don Lamoine was absolutely right about the problem we had. The shimmy dampener on the right inboard strut had failed, the rear dual engine pod hangars had failed and if we had fired the ATO it almost certainly would have resulted in some very dangerous maneuvers.

Kollsman Windows Tampered With

After take-off and climb out, the co-pilot reported through 31,000'. This was an impossibility due to the take-off weight and I corrected it, but the altimeters did read that. We were lucky to be able to reach 23-24,000' right after take-off. Obviously, some ground crew man had changed both altimeters so that they read 10,000' high. A crew had crashed into the mountains south of the base just before that, and were obviously way too low, probably had flown the entire mission 10,000 feet lower than expected.

To my knowledge no one ever investigated the circumstances surrounding the crash of the airplane with respect to the possibility of tampering or the report we made regarding the obvious tampering with the Kollsman window on the altimeters. It may have been that the aircraft was so crushed that nothing could be recovered. Our complaint, though, should have been investigated, since only a limited number of people had access to our airplane on the ground and it would not have been too hard to check it out.

"I don't fly with people who swear at me"

As mentioned above my early days of refueling with KC-97

tankers was sometimes hair-raising. I over-controlled and scared people. One night an instructor was in the back seat while I was diving at this KC-97 and kicking the hell out of the rudders, and he started calling me names and swearing at me, telling me how my ancestors were no good either. I told him he had the airplane and I took my hands off of the controls. He came back that he had not sworn at me and my navigator came over the interphone, "Oh yes you did, Major." Things calmed down after that and I did a better job.

"You've got 3 and 4, I've got the rest."

My old nemesis, the squadron ops officer rode with me one night to make some touch-and-go landings. He was not the smoothest pilot in the world and every time he got ready to take-off from the roll out on the runway, he just jammed the throttles forward and usually caused one or more of the engines to stall. He would call out, "You work out the stalls on 3 and 4, and I have the rest," and then away we would go. After a while I got tired of this and tried to avoid flying with him.

"Don't you have a job? You're too young to be retired!"

When we arrived in Tucson we rented a home in town. Almost immediately we purchased a lot and started building our own home. When the adobe walls were at plate level I took 30 days' leave, hired a carpenter and framed the house. I was constantly working outside when I could on all facets of getting a yard and driveway installed, plus painting everything paintable. Because of my schedule it seemed that I was always working on our house. A young pharmacist neighbor of ours stopped on day and asked me if I didn't have a job. I was 31 at the time and he said I was obviously too young to be retired. I told him I was in the Air Force and flew B-47s at Davis Monthan. He wouldn't believe me.

"You're under arrest!"

The co-pilot of a B-47 crew talked his aircraft commander into going hunting in the desert, to the east of Davis Monthan AFB. They had not shaved for a day or so, were in disreputable clothes and were armed when they suddenly found themselves approaching the Nuclear Weapons Storage area. The Security

Strategic Air Command

presents

Membership
in the
B-52 2000 Hour Club

CAPTAIN LYLE D. CLAWSON

to

For Outstanding Airmanship

AUTHENTICATED BY:

James McClellan
JAMES V. REARDON
Colonel, USAF

SAC FORM 280 PC: 1982.

Fig.14   Certificate — B-52 2000 Hour Club

people placed them under arrest and returned them to the Base. The aircraft commander wouldn't talk to the co-pilot afterwards because he felt that the co-pilot had embarrassed him beyond what he wanted to take in the way of ribbing from the other crews, and there was a crew change.

"Where did everyone go?"

There was a shortage of combat ready crews to pull ground alert and we were on a fast track to upgrade our new co-pilot, Captain Harry Ornelas. The last step was a weapons acceptance and alert start. The acceptance part of the check went smoothly. The alert start included an inspection of the bomb bay by the co-pilot and simulating pulling of the red Manual Locking Wrench, which was a positive prevention of a possible inadvertent release of the Nuclear Weapon on the ground. Harry was so damned nervous, he rushed into the bomb bay and actually pulled the red-handled wrench with a red flag hanging on it and left the bomb bay with it. Man, everyone left town in a hurry and I was in the cockpit wondering where the hell the co-pilot, was because I had the engines on the starboard side started! That was the end of the check. Harry's previous job in the Wing was Weapons Training Officer and he had gone through this with all the crews upgrading. Later that night I received a call from the Wing Stand board that if we would come back out to the base in a hurry, they would forget the previous try and give us another go at it. We did and passed. I always believed that the reason we go another chance was that the Stand board crew would have had to pull our alert slot if we didn't pass.

My crew was TDY to Guam for 45 days to pull alert. The Task Force Commander had the aircraft commanders come in to headquarters for a briefing. This was different and we were concerned about the content of he briefing. We were told that the 43rd Bomb Wing was moving to Fort Worth to acquire the new supersonic B-58's and that the B-47 crews were going en mass to B-52 training at Castle. This was the last kind of change that I wanted, but there was no way out, so we chose Rome, New York and started the upgrade process.

Chapter IV: B-52 Operational Bomb Wing

668TH BOMBARDMENT SQUADRON
GRIFFISS AFB, ROME, NY
MARCH 1960—MAY 1963

The dispersal of B-52 wings started in 1959 with what was termed a Strategic Wing. The typical strategic wing had a standard 15 B-52 configuration. The wing at Griffiss had been stationed at Limestone, Maine, until about a year prior to my arrival in 1960. Some units also had Tanker aircraft assigned. The 4039th Strategic Wing at Griffiss had an augmented tanker force because of its location along the bomber stream route to the Soviet Union. Originally the squadron was the 75th, later changed to the 668th. When I arrived at Griffiss I had missed my flight training and had to be rescheduled; therefore it was hard to find any meaningful work for my crew.

On January 1, 1961 it snowed 36" in twenty-four hours. Even the snow plows in Rome were unable to keep up with it, and they were masters at snow removal. Nothing moved and even the alert crews were sent home when they could get there. The base was simply shut down. We shoveled the snow out of our deep driveway and just as we finished the snow plows from the base came along and filled it up completely.

"If I call you an S.O.B...."

My first meeting with the Squadron Commander, Lt. Col. Willie Sonntag, went something like this: "Clawson, get your ass in my office, [which was a glassed-in enclosure]. I'm going to tell how I operate. If I feel like calling you a Son-of-a-Bitch, I will. If you tell anyone I called you an S. O. B., I'll call you a liar."

There was never any question of what Willie thought of you.

Because I did not have the flight training necessary to proceed on to combat readiness training, my crew and I were given many meaningless tasks. I started looking for a real job and since I had an FAA Engine and Power-plant Mechanic's license, the Deputy Commander for Maintenance (DCM) was interested in hiring me. When I met with him, the last thing he said was for me to be careful that Willie did not find out about our meeting.

Willie: "I won't speak to you for one week"

Willie caught me right after I had been to see the Deputy Commander for Maintenance (DCM), Colonel Brock, and raised hell with me. I was trying to get a meaningful job. I could never figure out how he knew I had seen Brock, but this was an indicator that he had spies everywhere. He said he would not speak to me for a week and then I was to come into his office and we'd have this out. After a week he had calmed down a little and told me that the main reason he did not want to see me work for Brock was that Brock had ruined the career of every officer that worked for him. I stayed in the squadron and really got to like Willie.

"SOME DAY SAC WILL RULE THE WORLD"

Just before I arrived at Griffiss AFB the Wing Commander came into possession of some matchbooks, plain white on the outside and on the inside in big bright letters were the words "SOME DAY SAC WILL RULE THE WORLD". These matchbooks had been circulating all over northern New York state. The Wing Commander declared a full recall of all personnel of the Wing and required them to produce all of the existing match books, which he confiscated. There was a big flap all the way up to SAC Headquarters and it was by the skin of his teeth that the WC survived this issue. The culprit was one of the crew gunners who had thousands of these things printed. The Wing Commander later became a Major General and considered this one of the hottest issues he had been involved in.

The gunner was reprimanded and promised not to repeat this performance and continued on a crew. The crew was later rotated to Ramey AFB in Puerto Rico. Guess what, the matchbooks reappeared shortly after his arrival in the islands… We never heard what might have been done to him, but as far as our Commander was concerned it could not have been enough.

B-52 GROUND ALERT

This was probably the most boring time of our duty on the B-52. There was very little to occupy our time. When I went to the alert facility for our week-long duty I had my own pillow, electric blanket and sheets. I was also one of very few captains enrolled in the Air War College correspondence course. Usually you had to be at least a major, but since I had completed all of the other "career enhancing" correspondence courses including the "Emergency Management of the National Economy " from the Industrial College of the Armed Forces, the War College let me in.

Many amusing things happened while we were on alert. The Tanker crews also shared the alert facility. The airmen pitched in with some really bizarre activities. No one ever spent much time figuring out who did what but sometimes it was almost self-evident which group did something.

Guys like Bill Brock made a lasting impression. He was really one of those unforgettable characters.

"Bullshit Your Way Out of This One, Brock!"

Captain Bill Brock was always in hot water with Willie Sonntag. He had been in a Tanker Squadron with Willie as the squadron commander. This was another day. The alert Bombers and Tankers were parked in two separated areas. If the active runway on a Bravo alert (taxi to active runway) was in one direction, the tankers went first; if the other direction was active, the Bombers taxied first. We would take the active in turn, apply full power and immediately reduce power to idle and taxi off the active. One day we had a Bravo alert and the Bombers were supposed to taxi first to the nearest runway. But Brock was in such a hurry, he always had a rubber band on the starter switch, so that when the ground crew applied power, the first engine started, usually just as the crew arrived. Brock taxied like hell to the other end of the runway, and was there alone. Everyone was back in the Alert Facility when he came in and Willie accosted him saying, "Well Brock, bullshit your way out of this one!" with everyone cheering.

What was the punchline, General?—Brock

Captain Bill Brock kept a journal of everything that went on. He claimed he would write a book about his experiences. When a "big shot" general or high-ranking civilian was visiting the Wing they would usually attend a briefing of the alert crews in the Alert Facility. They would usually try to break the ice with a filthy joke. Brock made it a habit of writing the joke down and then interrupting the visitor after he had delivered the punchline, with,

"General, would you repeat that, I missed it." This would sort of unnerve the visitor, knowing that his off-color joke was being recorded and attributed.

Request change of briefing time—Debbie Drake

Debbie Drake was a very attractive young lady who had an exercise program on TV every morning. The crews would gather in the lounge and, with the sound off, make unsavory remarks while she moved about. On the days we had briefings, the crews would miss Debbie, so we petitioned the DCO to change the briefing time, and he did.

Den Mother complains about paper in latrine

The Lt. Col. (Navigator) who was in charge of the Alert Facility was called the Den Mother. He was a prissy guy and fussed about everything. One morning at the briefing he went overboard fussing about the paper being left on the latrine floor and how messy it looked. The next morning he couldn't get the door open, the crews had stuffed the place full of any paper they could roll up.

Backfire in underground

Someone drove a Volkswagen Bug through the lower hallway of the Alert Facility and backfired just as it hit the bottom. Of course the crews, who were sound asleep, would have killed the guy if he were caught. It was on the hallway where the gunners slept.

On my schedule, I'll get even with you

One of my crew-members pulled a lousy trick on me, which sort of made me look like a fool to the others. I told him I would get even on my schedule. It would not be expected, and just look out... After about three weeks he came to me and said that he wanted the thing over, "Whatever you're going to do, do it, you're driving me nuts!" I told him that I had already done it. I had driven him nuts waiting for the shoe to fall.

"Challenge me"

Commercial power failure automatically sounded the "alert" alarm. The crews would respond to the klaxon and wait for the command post to instruct them on what type of alert it was. When the controller expressed surprise that all the aircraft were manned and engines going he said it was a mistake, shut down and go back to bed. The crews didn't go for that and wanted him to authenticate. His answer was, "Challenge me." This required him to go through the authentication process.

Bang, bang in Front of alert B-52s

Someone of the Alert crews had wired firecracker bombs on our Den Mother's Volkswagen Bug. As he left, he crossed the ramp right in front of the Alert B-52s, each with an armed Air Policeman in front of the aircraft. About halfway across the ramp the first loud report came from the car. Lots of attention, the car then proceeded, and after about another fifty feet another one exploded. Some people didn't think it funny, others of us thought it ingenious.

Flat outrigger gear on Alert Aircraft

One weekend day when we were on alert, we went to the airplane for some reason and saw that the right outrigger gear was flat and the rim was near or on the ramp. I got on the airplane and called the command post and informed them that we were not mission ready and take us off alert status.

Within a few minutes the Vice Wing Commander came out to the Alert Facility and told me to call the aircraft back on alert, that he had let the maintenance crews go home, and he had no one to change the tire. I explained that if we were to have a Bravo or higher alert I could not taxi because of the danger of fire. He said I was to hold my position if we had such and alert and give the times as if I had taxied. I refused and he got someone to change the tire. I heard no more about it.

Routine Training Missions

Once we had the twenty-two or three authorized crews combat ready and all pulling alert, we still had to meet quarterly training requirements. This meant that we pulled one-week ground alert and usually flew two missions the next week and then back in the hole. Sometimes we might get two weeks off alert, but that was because our Wing had an airborne alert requirement. The wing had a requirement for certifying that the crews were

90

not exceeding an average of 80 hours' duty per week. I don't know how they actually figured it, but most of the time we exceeded that number.

The following anecdotes have to do primarily with normal 8 to 10-hour training missions that normally involved refueling, night and day Navigation legs and low-level Navigation and simulated bombing missions. They were flown mostly at night. The missions could extend as far west as Texas and south to Florida. Many discrepancies were noted, both mechanically and with the crew training. All of these were debriefed in excruciating detail.

Near Miss—Idelwild Vortac

At high altitude in the 1950-1960 time frame, military aircraft flew what was termed hemispheric altitudes. This meant that depending which direction you were traveling you could choose odd or even and sometimes odd + 500' or even + 500'. Changes would usually be made as you changed headings over radio facilities or navigation leg changes. We were changing altitudes and heading over Idelwild Vortac when the airplane hit what was obviously jet wash from another aircraft and was knocked off the autopilot. The Lt. Col., who was climbing the stairs from the navigator compartment, was thrown down them and banged up. We immediately scanned the area and there was another B-52 also climbing and turning. The workload in the cockpit was distracting and even though everyone knew that clearing the area (making sure there was no conflicting traffic in the area) was most important, they failed to do it all the time. (see Davis Monthan—Near miss, minor damage.)

"Colonel, I'm not going one knot slower"

Willie and I were getting refueling portion of a Stand Board. Willie was first and fought with Brock the whole time over the speed the Tanker was going. Brock told he wouldn't go a knot slower because they had a defective tail section. Willie admonished Brock not to give Clawson a bad time with his refueling. Brock was on his way to Seattle, to deliver the KC-135 to the Boeing Plant to have the tail modified, and he would not accede to Willie's demand that he slow down more.

Albany to Rome Fighter Intercept

Following a training mission we were assigned a mission with the ADC fighters (F-89 Scorpions) stationed at Rome. We were to descend over Albany, New York, and depart the Vortac at 1,000 feet at a specific time and fly directly to Griffiss AFB. The ADC fighters were to scramble and intercept us. We departed within 10 seconds of the assigned time and followed our prescribed flight to Griffiss. At debriefing we caught hell for supposedly trying to mess up the Air Defense Command (ADC) mission by changing our flight path because they never saw us on radar and the fighters were not scrambled. Our logs were thoroughly checked and they showed that we complied exactly with our instructions for the mission and we were off the hook.

"Mr. Clawson, do you have anything to say?"

Our crew had been on leave and was scheduled for a training mission on the Monday we were to report back. This meant mission planning on Sunday, while still on leave, which was alright with us. We requested staff support for target study and mission planning, but the "staff weanies" were not about to come out to help us on Sunday. Naturally, the mission didn't go well and big bombs were thrown and the low level didn't go well, so when the debriefing came along all the "weanies" were there to criticize. Willie Sonntag was in good form and enjoying the hassling we were getting from the staff. When they had worn themselves out he looked at me and said "Well, *Mr*. Clawson, do you have anything to say?"

I banged on the desk with the chair in front of me so hard I thought it would break and said, "You're damn right I have!" For the next five minutes, I pointed at each of the "weanies" and said that we had asked for help during mission planning and they had not responded. When I slowed down some, Willie asked me if I had anything else to say, I said, "No Sir". He responded, "Take your motley crew and get the hell out of here."

I remember thinking at the time, that maybe I overdid it. About ten minutes later I was walking out of the building and went by an office with the door open and Willie was sitting at a desk with his feet up, and he called to me. "Hey Don, come on in, let's shoot the bull for a while."

B-52 Right Main Gear indicates unsafe

The first crew mission I flew without an IP in the B-52G was uneventful until we arrived over high station to begin our penetration to Griffiss AFB to terminate our mission. As we departed high station and started down, we put the landing gear handle in the down position. The right main showed an intermediate position, indicating the gear was not down and locked. We retracted the gear, received clearance to remain in holding pattern, recycled once—same thing, retracted all gear and remained in holding pattern. We contacted the SAC Command Post at Griffiss AFB and informed them of our problem. After the standard "standby" the controller, Capt. Royal T. Squires, came back with, "Have you performed all the steps in the emergency section on page 3-21 of the flight manual?" We were also informed that Eighth AF, our higher headquarters, had put a hold on our use of the "Hot Switch", which at times would override normal functions and allow the gear to go to a safe condition. But in the meantime we had already used it, got the gear down and were starting penetration. Next day I asked Squires what the business of procedures on page 3-21 was about, he said some one had removed those pages from the Command Post copy of the Flight Manual and the controllers knew the procedure for an unsafe landing gear was contained on that page.

"Jack-rabbit 47, You're Losing Parts off Your Right Wing"

The Boomer on a tanker over Cleveland area during refueling called us to say we were loosing parts off of our right wing. We dropped back to check the engines and it turned out that our number three engine (left wing) was bad, so we caged it. The Boomer was calling out the right wing as he saw it. The next day I went out on the ramp to see the airplane, and the Pratt & Whitney engine representative was there. I ask him what caused the engine to blow up. Boy, he said, P and W engines don't "blow up". About three weeks later a similar incident had occurred, so I went out to see how similar they were. The same guy looked at me and said, "What took you so long?"

Sadistic Planners—Refueling Track—Westbound—Cleveland

For some time we had a refueling track near Cleveland, Ohio, in the afternoon that put the tanker just slightly to the right of the sun and at the same elevation. Since most of the planners were navigators, I always contended that it was sadistic revenge for all the slights they felt they received from pilots. It was extremely difficult and somewhat dangerous.

Cape Cod entry for low level—Nav vomits, Soviets duck

We had one mission to fly low level out over the Atlantic departing Cape Cod and flying out several hundred miles and then returning to Maine to a bombing range where we would drop a blue devil. The "blue devil" was a small ballistic shape that had enough high explosive to mark the impact for scoring. Our nominal altitude was 500' but we were soon much lower. The co-pilot, a friend to all navigators, called to the Nav and asked him to come up and have a look. He did, threw up on the co-pilot, and ran back downstairs and strapped in.

The radar navigator would call out that we were approaching ships and for a few minutes we could not see them, they were over our horizon. As we approached them we could see that they were Soviet Spy Trawlers. We would pull up enough to clear the ship but can you image what it sounded like on the ship as we passed. Approaching we could not see anyone on deck, but I'll bet there were a few of them on deck after we passed.

"Why the hell did you break the airplane, Colonel?"

Colonel Sonntag, by now full colonel and Deputy Commander for Operations (DCO), was the aircraft commander on a B-52 mission that had the front gear spring break as he started to taxi and the gear spread and wrecked the tires. As soon as the word got to the alert facility we all got in our vehicles to go cheer Willie on. I got close to him and said, "What the hell did you do that for, Colonel? I won't repeat what he said to me in response.

"You and your Crew are to be Commended"

Typical of the military, we were not kept very busy on alert, so the staff thought it would be good if they required each crew to create

Fig.15   EC-121 College Eye crew on Taiwan (Author kneeling next to sign on left)

a study guide for the Wing Emergency War Order. The Navigator on my crew was a Naval Academy graduate and former professor of English at the Air Force Academy. He took over the project and we all stood back and watched. He typed a title page, index, forward and first page of text and the rest of the thirty pages had "this page intentionally left blank". We turned it in and never heard any thing about it until I got my next evaluation and there was a very nice commendation regarding the hard work we did on the study guide. I passed on the commendation in each of the crew-members officer effectives report (OER) and we all had a good laugh. If Willie had ever read what we turned in, he'd have shot us.

Sorry, Sir...

Captain John Adelman, Navigator (NAV) treated the Gunner very poorly. The gunner managed to accidentally spill coffee on the floor upstairs and it ran down the Nav's neck for most of the mission. He later tilted the carrier for the very heavy thermos jugs in such a fashion as to allow one thermos to slip through the basket and hit the Nav on the foot. It really hurt for the entire mission and the gunner never did apologize.

> *One of the items concerning the crews that were going to strike targets in the Soviet Union or its allies was the exit from the target area after all the weapons had been dropped. A scenario was always briefed and sometimes the crews thought another direction would be safer. The briefer would invariably say it is up to us, which way we turned. We do not expect to recycle your aircraft and after bombs away you are working for yourself.*
>
> *One such scenario that was briefed was a recovery that would take us down over North Africa, landing at an unattended runway complex that would have fuel in 55-gallon barrels with a hand pump to load fuel on the aircraft. The biggest problem here was that there would be no auxiliary power or air carts to start the engines. This required that we keep one engine running for air. The discussion got around to the fact that the hand pump would not even keep up with the requirement to run one engine. We didn't care for their scenario.*
>
> *It was quite obvious that no one thought there would be a need for such a runway and we all doubted that there was any fuel there either.*

CHROME DOME MISSIONS

Starting in 1962 the Wing was assigned Chrome Dome missions, which were B-52s on airborne alert with war reserve chaff, ammunition and nuclear weapons along with decoy missiles on board and ready for use. These missions usually lasted over 23 hours and included two refuelings over Spain of approximately 126,000 lbs each, which took approximately 26 minutes contact time to receive. We soon found out that it was essential to your comfort, once you strapped in, not to wiggle. If you wiggled, it was one cheek and the other for the entire mission. We got to the point that it was 5 or 6 hours to the first wiggle.

"Why don't you take the bombs off, then?"

I had an exchange with Willie Sonntag about briefing non-combat ready crew-members flying relief positions on Chrome Dome missions. Willie did not want to have to brief non-ready crew-members on the use of the escape and evasion "Blood Chit" and other procedures for downed crew-members. He told me that we weren't going anywhere near the Soviet Union—it was a drill. I told that if that were the case, why didn't we simulate the weapons and take the real ones off? I got the crew-members briefed.

B-52 AIRBORNE ALERT—CUBAN MISSILE CRISIS

In researching archives, published books, oral histories and discussions with officers who were serving in high positions, it is evident that very little has been recorded regarding the command and control of the airborne alert B-52's. High-ranking SAC officers always made a big issue of the fact that they didn't want to use the term 'command, control and communications' because they had no forces that they commanded that they didn't control. In the case of the Airborne Alert B-52s, they did not possess the capability to prevent a rogue crew or crew-member from arming and releasing their thermonuclear weapons. They also did not possess the capability of preventing the same or other rogue crew or crew-member from constructing and broadcasting a message on high frequency radio that would have executed the entire Airborne Alert force without possibility of recall. The crews had all of the information for this hanging around each of the three primary crew-members' necks. Positive control did not exist without the crews' acquiescence. This situation lasted for the entire time I flew Chrome

Dome missions.

What I am saying is that once the crew was airborne, with in my case six thermonuclear weapons, two Hound Dog missiles and four Quail drones, it would have been possible to arm and drop them all with no further input from the ground. There was no inhibitor on any of the systems.

The reason I am making this point is that the crews flying 23 to 25-hour missions all over the world with the most lethal load of weapons ever imagined were never acknowledged for what they did. Their integrity was all that kept the world from going up in flames. The citizens of the Soviet Union will never understand how much they owe to these 60 to 176 crews that flew every day, refueling with not so perfect aircraft in some of the worst weather and turbulence imaginable. The force flying over Spain was scheduled and conducted 48 huge refuelings each 24 hours of 120,000+ pounds each, with not one abort. This accomplishment by each crew was at least meritorious and in many cases extraordinary—which should have earned many of them Air Medals and Distinguished Flying Crosses. To my knowledge not one was ever given.

The US National Command Authority believed that there was 1/8 of the B-52 force flying Airborne Alert. Nikita Kruschev believed that 20% of the force was on airborne alert. General David A. Burchinal, at that time Director of Plans on the Air Staff at Air Force Headquarters, says that we had 1/3 of the force in the air. This equates to at least 60 aircraft in the air all of the time for 1/8, and 176 for 1/3. This meant as many as 616 large yield thermonuclear weapons were being flown all over the northern hemisphere, controlled mainly by captains and majors. There were some lieutenant colonels, most of who were spot promoted, and their permanent or temporary rank was major. Most of these officers were products of the Air University's Squadron Officers School of the middle 1950s where Major General Orvil Anderson, USAF (Retired) and former Commandant of the Air War College, lectured each class regarding the evils of the Soviet Union. He specifically called for bombing the Soviets with nuclear weapons, not tomorrow, but tonight…

From perusing the 18,000 plus pages of the declassified material held by the National Security Archives on the Cuban Missile Crisis, it is evident that the National Command Authority (NCA) knew very little about the circumstances of the B-52 Airborne Alert.

The additional force was undoubtedly not known to the NCA, just as the order putting the entire SAC force in Defcon 2 was unknown to the NCA until after the fact. Defcon 2 was the highest state of alert ever reached by SAC. Defcon 1 would have meant the shooting had started. The transcript of the JCS chronology of events does not reflect any change in force structure on Airborne Alert until the order went out to stand down *from the 1/8 Airborne Alert.*

I have queried Mr. Robert S. McNamara, Secretary of Defense at the time, whether he was aware of the uninhibited weapons on the B-52s and that the crews could have executed the entire force and as we expected; he did not respond. My letter is included in the addendum. Also I queried the Defense Attaché at the Russian Confederation Embassy in Washington as to whether their "listeners" knew what to look for as far as a command to the B-52s to proceed to their targets; again, as expected, no response.

We were damned lucky we didn't blow up the world—and no thanks to the political or military leadership of this country.

"Date and time, you are not cleared to take the runway "

Our crew was on ground alert when the Cuban Missile Crisis was initially brewing. Lots of activity, as the entire squadron was put on alert, with weapons and fuel uploaded. The afternoon of October 24, 1962, the DCO, Colonel Willie Sonntag, instructed me to get my crew to bed early the evening before the first Chrome Dome (CD) mission was to fly, because we were to be the back-up crew to fly. The Chrome Domes we had flown before never aborted since there was total maintenance support for each mission. We used to laugh about the amount of spare parts the maintenance people had in the trucks on the ramp. The regulations called for the maintenance people to keep all spare parts at a central point. Those guys had enough parts to build a B-52 right on the ramp. As luck would have it, the scheduled CD crapped out and we had to take our squadron commander as the third pilot—even though he could not refuel—and fly the mission. As we taxied out to the runway for take-off on October 25, 1962, the Thule Monitor (TM) landed with an emergency, which automatically closed the runway until the Airdrome Officer (AO) could inspect the runway for foreign objects. "Old Nickle Nose", the Wing Commander (WC) was in his staff car right next to our aircraft and in contact with us on the Command Post frequency. The tower repeated several times the date and time and the instruction, "You are not clear to take the runway nor to take-off" then the date/time group again.

The WC instructed me to go. "Clawson, get out of here, now". I recalled an old SAC adage that the Commander-in-Chief, SAC was god and your wing commander was his son. I was not for one second going to argue that the Control Tower says I can't do it. We took the active runway and as soon as TM cleared it we took off, all the time hearing the tower saying we were not cleared for take-off. The reason the WC was so adamant was that the window for our crossing the Atlantic was almost closed and the mission would have to have been scrubbed.

Lots of threats, we heard, between Air Traffic Control Headquarters in Texas and the WC, each threatening courts martial, but we never heard a thing officially about the incident. The nation was closest to Nuclear War on October 26, 1962 that we have ever been. We landed about noon of the 26th.

I claim the distinction of being the only pilot in the world who ever took the active runway and took off with six thermonuclear weapons on board while the tower was ordering him not to take the active runway and that he was not cleared for take-off.

During the time the Airborne Alert aircraft was in flight there were people interested in our flight other than SAC command elements. Malta Control always asked for our departure point and destination. We never answered their query.

On each of the CD flights before the Cuban Crisis when we flew the southern route through the Mediterranean, the electronics warfare officer always indicated that we were being illuminated in some way from an airborne platform behind us, once we paralleled the north coast of Africa, until we turned back west near Tripoli. This led us to believe that once we arrived in the Mediterranean Sea we were under some sort of surveillance by an aircraft.

"You'll have to stand by, we are in the middle of a shift change"

Returning from a CD we climbed to 41,000 feet while southeast of Boston, and as we approached the Air Defense Identification Zone (ADIZ) we called the Air Defense Command command post per standard operating procedure (SOP), and could not get a response. We tried several channels and came back to the assigned channel and called some more. A disgusted voice came on the air and said we would have to stand by, they were in the middle of a shift change. Here was a large bomber, with no track number assigned yet, with nuclear weapons on board, approaching

Boston, and we were put on hold!

"Doc, you have to see what the crews are enduring"

The Wing Commander had told the Flight Surgeon (FS) assigned to our squadron that he should fly a Chrome Dome to see what the crews were enduring. He didn't want any part of it and so ignored the hint. The WC issued a written order for the FS to fly a CD; he complied and flew with our crew. After 24 hours of flight, we landed at Griffiss and he looked like a ghost. He never flew a CD again. One of the issues about the nutrition of the crews was raised on the mission. One of the staples on each mission was cup cakes. I was never very crazy about them, but got use to them after a couple of missions.

Thule Monitor—Prime Reason Given for the Mission

The official rationale for the Thule Monitor flights (which were really Chrome Dome missions) was that we would be able to notify SAC and Looking Glass (the SAC airborne command post) if Soviet missiles had taken out the early warning system at Thule, Greenland. Prime means of communication was UHF through Thule ground station with back-up by HF radio. Neither of these means would be available in the event of a detonation of a nuclear weapon. So much for that well thought-out plan.

The Thule Monitor mission was not quite as long as the regular Chrome Dome mission, but there was only one refueling and it was not as heavy as the ones over Spain. This was due to the distance the Tanker had to travel. This meant that we were always quite close to using our reserves for returning to a closed-in north-east base such as Griffiss. One night when the weather was a definite factor, the Thule Monitor crew returned to Griffiss and it was touch and go getting in because of the low ceilings and visibility. The aircraft commander, a major, took his wings off and threw them on the squadron commanders desk the next day and said he quit. I left about that time, and do not know whether he went through with his resignation or not.

When did the fuel leak first occur?

During the Cuban Missile Crisis, SAC had a special B-52 monitoring the area around Thule, Greenland, 24 hours a day.

These aircraft were Chrome Dome configured. One of our missions was scheduled for 22 hours and included one refueling with a Tanker from Elmendorf AFB, Alaska. Take-off and climb out was normal, the co-pilot was conducting a check of the fuel panel and mentioned that something was wrong, one tank feeding the left inboard pod was much lower than the corresponding tank on the starboard side. On the B-52G the gunner's station was in the upper aft forward section of the aircraft with the Electronic Warfare Officer (EW). He immediately turned on his TV and reported that we had a cloud coming off the left wing. I turned to see a large-diameter hose of fuel going a couple of feet straight down before breaking off into the slipstream. We shut the engine down and continued the mission. Hours later when we pulled up behind the KC-135 we were already below the predicted fuel remaining curve, and the Boomer informed us that he was unable to get the Boom out of the stowed position. Since ostensibly the mission was to monitor the Thule situation and inform SAC in the event of a nuclear attack, if the Bomber could not continue the mission, the Tanker had to remain in the Thule area until relieved by the next Bomber. This was a great incentive for the Tanker crew to work hard to supply the Bomber with fuel. We had informed the Tanker that in 30 seconds we were breaking off the formation and returning to Base. Just then the boom came down, we refueled, completed the mission and returned to Griffiss. Approximately 200 miles out we contacted the Command Post and informed them that we had a fuel leak and had shut the engine down. They immediately wanted to know when the leak occurred. We informed them that it had just started.

During maintenance debriefing, we were hounded by a lieutenant who wanted to know exactly when the leak occurred. We never changed our story. The reason was that we were within UHF range of Eighth Air Force at Westover AFB, Massachusetts, when the leak occurred, and had we informed our command post they would have had no choice but to have us stay local, burn off fuel and land. Willie would have killed me.

The Thule Monitor mission was truly unique; we would arrive over Thule, turn to the east and fly two hundred miles.

Fig.16   Notional version of wing emblem –
Tribute to Robert McNamara

Fig.17   EC-121-R Bat Cat Crew (Author kneeling third from left)

During certain times of the year the sun would go down, when we turned to fly back to Thule the sun would "come up" in the west.

Request Permission to Shoot

On Chrome Dome missions to the Mediterranean we had two refuelings over Spain. The first was about seven hours after take-off and the second about fourteen hours. After the second refueling I usually had the relief pilot take my position and I would go to sleep on a cot behind the pilots. This day I did just that. When I was sound asleep, the two co-pilots were throwing their helmets at me to wake me. I went forward and they explained that two Spanish Air Force F-86s were on our tail, and had not come up on our left wing to be identified as they should have, so the Gunner had slewed his guns on them and locked on. He requested permission to shoot. The American GCI sites were calling our aircraft on Guard Channel telling us not to shoot at them, they were just sergeants and didn't know what they were doing. We were not far from Madrid. Shooting down a couple of Spanish fighters near their capital I am sure would not have gone over very well.

Incredible reliance on Crew integrity

The total reliance on the B-52 combat crew force's integrity amazes me even today. Obviously if the crew had the ability to deconstruct and verify a simple, in the clear message, they also had the ability to construct a valid message. Each aircraft had the means of transmitting such a message that would only require authentication to execute the entire Airborne Alert Force, with no recall possible. The crews spent hours becoming familiar with all facets of "Positive Control", the so-called Fail Safe Doctrine, and were experts in validating all types of messages.

In spite of the contention shown in motion pictures such as *Dr. Strangelove* and *Thirteen Days* that there was an electronic interlock on the B-52 inhibiting the crew from arming and dropping the weapons, there was no such system. All the crew needed was a message in the proper format and authenticated with material hanging around each of the primary crew-members' neck's. It is instructive, when perusing the declassified documents from the Cuban Crisis period, that very little is said about the control procedures for the Airborne Alert of the B-52 force. This archive contains more than 18,000 pages of documents. There are also inconsistencies in the documents. It is obvious that SAC conducted many operations not disclosed to the National Command Authority (civilian).

A rogue crew or crew-member could have easily and quickly composed an authentic message and broadcast it on HF radio, which would have required all SAC elements to keep re-broadcasting it. There was a two-man policy in effect requiring two people be in one place at a time when the activity involved nuclear weapons, but when flying Airborne Alert, we sometimes did not have a third pilot, which meant that there was frequently only one pilot in the cockpit when the other was sleeping. The crews were fully aware of this situation; in fact we discussed it from time to time. Only one crew-member was known to be armed and everyone knew who had the gun, so he could have been taken out easily.

The crews were required to become experts in Positive Control procedures after an incident in 1959 when the newly activated combat-ready refueling squadron at Castle AFB launched their alert Tankers on the word of an enlisted man in the command post. A command element person drove his vehicle in the path of a Tanker to stop the launch of the rest of the squadron. It was clear that the crews and the command element did not understand the Positive Control problem. The Wing Commander got on the radio and ordered the airborne crews to return. Some did return, although in actual practice there would not have been a recall. Some turned off their radios and went to their rendezvous points and orbited, waiting for their bombers, until they had to land for reasons of low fuel. There was a massive change in training following this incident. (*See Goodfellow for General Anderson's remarks at Squadron Officer's School- Last quarter of 1955*)

Roma Control threatens

Rome Air Traffic Control was impossible to reach by radio, UHF or HF. We would try every frequency in the book time and again

Fig.18　EC-121-R Aircraft in flight

I. IDENTIFICATION DATA (Read AFM 36-10 carefully before filling out any item.)

1. LAST NAME—FIRST NAME—MIDDLE INITIAL	2. AFSN	3. ACTIVE DUTY GRADE	4. PERMANENT GRADE
Brown, Thomas S.	569-3º-2678FR	Major	Major

5. ORGANIZATION AND COMMAND	6. AERO RATING	CODE	7. PERIOD OF REPORT
553 Recon Sq Korat RTAFB, Thailand (PACAF)	Sr Nav	1	FROM 11 Aug 69 THRU 9 Dec 69

8. PERIOD OF SUPERVISION	9. REASON FOR REPORT
121	CRO

II. DUTIES—PAFSC 1525Z **DAFSC** 1535Z PRESENT DUTY: Sq Navigator, EC-121R. Maintains combat ready status in an around-the-clock all weather reconnaissance operation. Plans missions, performs preflight inspections, provides necessary forms and publications prior to flight. Monitors clearances received by pilot, maintains accurate inflight position. Identifies equipment malfunctions and supervises proper corrective actions. Plots and logs essential intelligence information. Assists aircraft commander in crew supervision as directed. ADDITIONAL DUTIES: Squadron Stan/Eval Navigator, Squadron Navigator.

III. RATING FACTORS (Consider how this officer is performing on his job.)

1. JOB CAPABILITY
2. PLANNING ABILITY
3. EXECUTIVE MANAGEMENT
4. LEADERSHIP
5. EXECUTIVE JUDGMENT
6. HUMAN RELATIONS
7. WRITING ABILITY AND ORAL EXPRESSION
8. JOB ACCOMPLISHMENT

IV. MILITARY QUALITIES (Consider how this officer meets Air Force standards.)

AF FORM 707 PREVIOUS EDITION OF THIS FORM WILL BE USED UNTIL STOCK IS EXHAUSTED.

FIELD GRADE OFFICER EFFECTIVENESS REPORT

Fig.19　Major Thomas Brown's Officer Effectiveness Report

V. OVER-ALL EVALUATION (Compare this officer ONLY with officers of the same grade)

Specific justification required for these sections								Specific justification required for these sections
☐ UNSATIS-FACTORY	☐ MARGINAL	☐ BELOW AVER-AGE	☐ SLIGHTLY BE-LOW AVERAGE	☐ EFFECTIVE AND COMPETENT	☐	☐ EFFECTIVE-NESS WELL ABOVE MOST	☐ EXCELLENT, SELDOM EQUALED	☐ OUTSTANDING, ALMOST NEVER EQUALED	☒ ABSOLUTELY SUPERIOR

VI. PROMOTION POTENTIAL

1. DOES NOT DEMONSTRATE A CAPABILITY FOR PROMOTION AT THIS TIME ☐	2. PERFORMING WELL IN PRESENT GRADE. SHOULD BE CONSIDERED FOR PROMOTION ALONG WITH CONTEMPORARIES ☐
3. DEMONSTRATES CAPABILITY FOR INCREASED RESPONSIBILITY. CONSIDER FOR ADVANCEMENT AHEAD OF CONTEMPORARIES ☐	4. OUTSTANDING GROWTH POTENTIAL BASED ON DEMONSTRATED PERFORMANCE. PROMOTE WELL AHEAD OF CONTEMPORARIES ☒

VII. COMMENTS

FACTS AND SPECIFIC ACHIEVEMENTS: Major Brown is an absolutely superior officer who pursues each task with vigor and enthusiasm. His flawless navigational talents coupled with his superior knowledge of equipment and standard operating procedures resulted in his being appointed as Squadron Navigator and Squadron Stan/Eval Navigator. He has full responsibility for all navigation activities in the squadron. He discharges these responsibilities in an exceptional manner. He actively supervises the complete indoctrination of newly assigned navigators. His rigid adherence to operational and safety standards in this area materially enhance the unit's capability to accomplish its mission. He has continually evaluated charts, procedures and techniques, and has recommended updated procedures which have been adopted by the Wing for use as standard procedures. He works closely and in harmony with his counterpart on the Wing Stan /Eval Team. By establishing rapport with the Wing Stan/Eval Navigator and assisting in the writing of the Wing's operational procedures contained in several publications, effective coordination has been realized and the combat potential of the squadron has been increased. STRENGTHS: Major Brown thrives on an ever increasing scope of responsibility, brings exceptional insight to every problem presented and completes each task in a unique and professional manner. SUGGESTED ASSIGNMENT: Major Brown should be afforded every opportunity possible to return to the Communications and Electronics field at the highest command position commensurate with his grade. SELF IMPROVEMENT EFFORTS: During the period of this report, Major Brown has completed the Industrial College of the Armed Forces correspondence course. OTHER COMMENTS: All the above activities have been accomplished in addition to the demanding duties of a Combat Crew Evaluator flying in an actual combat environment. He has completed 64 combat missions and over 704 flying hours in Southeast Asia. The provisions of AFM 35-16 Special Career Monitoring apply to this officer.

VIII. REPORTING OFFICIAL

NAME, GRADE, AFSN, AND ORGANIZATION	DUTY TITLE	SIGNATURE	
LYLE D. CLAWSON, Major 552-26-9095FG, 553 Recon Sq Korat RTAFB, Thailand (PACAF)	Chief, Stan/Eval		
	AERO RATING: Command Pilot	CODE: 1	DATE: 9 December 1969

IX. REVIEW BY INDORSING OFFICIAL

I concur with this report except for Section III, Item 3, which I have initialed. Major Brown has not been involved in duties requiring extensive skills in executive management. In all other respects his performance has been superior.

NAME, GRADE, AFSN, AND ORGANIZATION	DUTY TITLE	SIGNATURE	
THOMAS E. DOYLE, Lt Colonel 545-05-6999FR, 553 Recon Sq Korat RTAFB, Thailand (PACAF)	Commander		
	AERO RATING: Command Pilot	CODE: 1	DATE: 9 December 1969

(CHECK APPROPRIATE BLOCK AND COMPLETE AS APPLICABLE)

☒ SUPPLEMENTAL SHEET TO RATING FORM WHICH COVERS THE FOLLOWING PERIOD OF REPORT

☐ LETTER OF EVALUATION COVERING THE FOLLOWING PERIOD OF OBSERVATION

FROM	THRU	FROM	THRU
11 Aug 69	9 Dec 69		

Precede comments by appropriate data, i.e. section continuation; indorsement continuation, additional indorsement, etc. Follow comments by the authentication to include: name, grade, AFSN, organization, duty title, date and signature.

ADDITIONAL INDORSEMENT

I do not concur with the report as changed by the indorsing official. I am personally aware of the superior and highly skilled manner in which Major Brown has applied his technical and managerial talents to train and qualify the limited squadron navigator resources to sustain the superior effectiveness of the Wing's combat mission requirements. His highly conscientious, professional attitude and his outstanding navigational skill indicate a high potential for positions of much greater responsibility. I recommend his consideration for early promotion to the grade of lieutenant colonel.

JOHN W. MITCHELL, Colonel, 041-14-3121FR, 553d Reconnaissance Wing, Commander, 9 Dec 69

AF FORM 77a SEP 68 PREVIOUS EDITION OF THIS FORM WILL BE USED UNTIL 30 JUN 69. AFTER THIS DATE, PREVIOUS EDITIONS WILL BE OBSOLETE.

SUPPLEMENTAL SHEET TO AF FORMS 77, 707, 909, 910, 911 AND 475

* U.S. GOVERNMENT PRINTING OFFICE: 1968 O-323-675

but no answer. We then had briefings that if we did not report to "Roma Control", they were going to bar us from their controlled airspace. One night I had used up all the frequencies for Roma Control when out of the blue a call came from Cagliari Approach Control in Sardinia. I asked him if he would pass a report to Roma Control, he agreed to and I asked him how he read my transmission and he came back with "Hunky dory." This meant that he could hear our transmission clearly. Until that minute I never knew where that phrase originated. He was my Roma Control contact from then on.

Meritorious and extraordinary achievement in Flight

By almost any account the B-52 crews flying the Airborne Alert missions were accomplishing an extremely demanding and difficult task by taking responsibility for the thermonuclear weapons and missiles on their aircraft and flying halfway around the world. The achievement went almost unnoticed. I do not remember one time of being encouraged by any ranking officer or civilian for what we did during period of the Cuban Missile Crisis. Even the archives are devoid of any mention of the extraordinary effort and accomplishments of these crews. We were later given Air Medals and Distinguished Flying Crosses for much less effort or skill in South-east Asia.

I flew 15 Chrome Dome missions, which was all I could because of the times we were assigned the mission. The total time in the air was in excess of 350 hours during which time we crossed the Atlantic Ocean 22 times and refueled 26 times taking on more than 2.5 million pounds of fuel in some of the worst weather possible. This did become somewhat routine, but in reflecting on what we were paid and the conditions we worked under, the reward was, "you can keep on doing it". We were gathered together in the squadron to listen to a pep talk and were reminded that it was not only monetary rewards we received, but there was a psychic income that we were not counting. Someone asked how much of this we could use to buy the kids shoes.

Only 60,000 pounds to go

The second refueling on a Chrome Dome over Spain was sometimes during daylight. This time it was daylight and very rough clear air turbulence. We usually just pulled up, plugged in and 26 minutes later disconnected with little or no conversation. This time the Tanker crew had requested a change of altitude several times but the Spanish Controllers would not allow the change, so we had to proceed with the refueling. The two aircraft were like corks in the ocean; sometimes we would be way above the Tanker, and steep banks above and below them. After about twenty disconnects, I queried the Boomer as to how much fuel we had to go, he replied, "Only 60,000 pounds to go"—roughly one half of our required load. Even the smart-ass co-pilot said he was sure glad he didn't have to get the fuel that day. I was double wringing wet when we finally disconnected for the last time.

Can I tell them about our hydraulic problem?

On one of our many Chrome Dome missions, we lost the use of the inboard hydraulic systems. This technically meant we could not refuel and would have had to land in Morocco. We didn't do this because we were expected to exert ourselves to complete the mission. There were times when crews looked for any excuse to cut a mission short. Some crews seldom returned to their base in one mission, mine never aborted a Chrome Dome mission. So I went through the two refuelings and continued our hourly Operations Normal reports to Eighth Air Force on HF. After we had completed all of our extra activities, the co-pilot asked if he could tell Eighth about our hydraulic problem. He did, it was about midnight in Rome NY on a Sunday night. When we returned Willie gave us hell because he figured that we knew what time it was when we called and they got him up to confer on actions to be taken. We flew back to Rome, New York.

Old co-pilot—Gissy Changed to new format

My regular co-pilot had been sent to Squadron Officer's School at Maxwell AFB and a new co-pilot had been assigned to the crew. When the Cuban Missile Crisis occurred the school was closed and the students returned to their bases. My crew flew quite frequently because the Wing had determined that some crews never made it back across the Atlantic in one try and others always did. We were the latter, so flew often. The co-pilot returning from Squadron Officer School (SOS) was assigned to my crew and we were all happy about that because he was a good trooper. One night we received a message telling us to change the authentication package, which we termed the "Gissy". The authentication package contained the classified information necessary to authenticate a "go code" or any other instructions sent to the airplane crew. It was in a new format from what it had been before he left for school. All of the rest of the crew knew this but Charlie got pretty upset until he finished checking it out.

Ocean Station Fixes—"Not Us"

The first navigator we had on the crew at Griffiss was not the best in the world. He would have us on headings of 180 degrees and 360 degrees crossing the Atlantic to Spain. Whenever we called for an Ocean Station fix, whatever they gave us, he would claim that it wasn't us. But he could generally get us within 200 miles of Santiago TACAN on the north-west coast of the Iberian Peninsula, and that satisfied our requirement for transiting the Atlantic.

General Officer flying KC-135 out of Moron

On one of our Chrome Dome flights during the Cuban fracas we were pulling up on a Tanker out of Moron, Spain, and I usually asked the pilot of the Tanker to turn certain lights off because they were annoying. I made my request and he turned every light on the airplane off. After a few words we got that straightened out and then he started extra maneuvering the Tanker, which made it more difficult. After some more time and about when we would have finished, all the no flow lights came on the fuel panel indicating that the tanker had ceased transferring the fuel. The co-pilot called "Break!" and we fell behind the Tanker. The Tanker pilot said we still had some fuel to receive and wanted to know if we wanted to hook up again. By this time we had enough fuel to complete the mission and had more than enough of this clown's flying, and I told him to clear the track and leave us.

When we debriefed, I told Willie that this guy should be straightened out. Two days later Willie said, "Forget it, he was a general." Later other crews told me he had done worse things to them and they had offered to land at Moron and have it out with him on the ramp.

Request for Weather at Rome, New York

Flying Chrome Dome missions through the Mediterranean was of interest to many people. Malta suspiciously always wanted to know our point of departure and destination. We never responded. We would ask for weather at Griffiss AFB, using the classified name for Rome. Even the Air Force weather people at Moron AB would come back with, "The weather at Griffiss AFB on your arrival will be…" So much for security.

"Land on the end of the runway"

Returning from a Chrome Dome, we had climbed to 41,000 feet prior to coasting in over the Boston area, we called the command post with an estimated time of arrival (ETA). Willie got on the radio and told us not to descend, they were probably going to divert us. We told him the weather was so clear we could see the base from where we were (we couldn't really, but it was clear). He told us that they had experienced a lot of rain and it had it had frozen and the whole place was a skating rink. We just happened to have the Vice Wing Commander on board and he wanted to go home, so he talked to Willie. Willie came back on to me and said, "Land on the end of the runway—if you're not happy with it, get the hell out of here!"

Of course the end of the runway is reserved for take-offs, not landing, which is normally 1500 feet from the approach end of the runway. But to comply with Willie's instructions and to get the Colonel home, we put the airplane down right on the end of the runway. The smart-ass co-pilot told me it was the first time he ever thought I knew what I was doing. We rolled the entire length of the runway before stopping and then had to wait 30 minutes for a tug to pull us back to the ramp.

SOME HUMOROUS HAPPENINGS, AND SOME NOT

Controversy over Skybolt and Hound Dog Missile Systems

The Hound Dog Air-to-Surface missile was a very unreliable weapon and everyone knew it. In fact we were constantly told that it was in interim weapon and that the Skybolt was going to replace it shortly. In the meantime, in good old fashion SAC fashion, the crews were required to

DEPARTMENT OF THE AIR FORCE
HEADQUARTERS 3902D AIR BASE WING (SAC)
OFFUTT AIR FORCE BASE, NEBRASKA, 68113

REPLY TO
ATTN OF: BDCOA

3 1 MAR 1970

SUBJECT: Outstanding Performance During Flight Examination

TO: SAC (DITD)

1. On 11 March 1970, Major Lyle D. Clawson, attached to this organization for flying, achieved the status of Highly Qualified as the result of superior airmanship during his initial qualification as T-29 first pilot.

2. This status can be achieved only through near perfect scores in testing and noncritical flight check areas, and perfect performance in fourteen critical flight check areas.

3. Fewer than 10% can be expected to achieve Highly Qualified status on recurring checks; those who have done so during initial qualification within the past several years may be counted on the fingers of one hand.

4. Major Clawson is to be complimented on his performance as a professional aviator. I am pleased to have him flying our aircraft.

Edward A. Crouchley

EDWARD A. CROUCHLEY, Colonel, USAF
Commander

1st Ind (DIT)   1 Apr 70

TO: Major Lyle D. Clawson

It is always a pleasure to indorse correspondence of this nature. I would also like to add my compliments to those of Colonel Crouchley for a job well done. I am sure you will bring the same professionalism to your new job as you demonstrated during your flight examination.

Edwin T. Yeoman

EDWIN T. YEOMAN, Col., USAF
Director of Targets
DCS/Intelligence

Peace . . . . is our Profession

Fig.20   One of few Attaboys

accomplish reliable results with it by the old-fashioned way—cheat. We always laughed about how easy it was to qualify navigators and radar navigators by doing their work legitimately. The results weren't always too good, though. The long lead time in training was in teaching them how to back in good results and not get caught.

The Chief of the Wing Standardization and Evaluation, a spot promoted Lieutenant Colonel, was overly conscientious and finally had enough of the requirement put on the crews by the Wing Commander to produce reliable results with the Hound Dog missile. Out of desperation and lack of smarts, he wrote and mailed two letters accusing the Wing Commander of cheating on results of Hound Dog Missions. One went to Headquarters, USAF Air Inspector and the other to the SAC Air Inspector at Omaha. The letters arrived on a Friday and it was said that it was standing room only at Wing Headquarters on Monday morning.

In accordance with standard operating procedures, the former spot lieutenant colonel, now a major, was scooped up and sent to the loony bin at the hospital for evaluation. We heard that this is normal treatment for anyone who questions the authority of his commander.

When Skybolt was cancelled in December, 1962, things got serious. We were told, no more cheating with Hound Dogs. If the missile malfunctioned or would not perform correctly, write it up and let maintenance work on it. The maintenance people started marrying each missile to one aircraft. Several crews flew one of these and got terrible results. A crew who had been on leave and had not heard the "no cheating" edict went out and got reliable runs and they thought the world had come down on them. I remember that the aircraft commander (A/C) saying that they had been the only ones to get a reliable bomb run on the missiles and couldn't understand what all the fuss was about. He was somewhat chagrined when told of the new edict.

Looked like a Neon Sign

During he Cuban Crisis we flew the Chrome Dome mission through the Strait of Gibraltar and up the west coast of Portugal before turning westerly to cross the Atlantic to return to base. One night the static electricity built up on the windscreen was spectacular. The Wing Flying Safety Officer, a Lt. Col., was in the right seat and the co-pilot was supposed to relieve him. The Colonel really wanted to get out of the seat because he was uncomfortable with all the lights. No one could raise the co-pilot and later he said he looked up and saw the windscreen and he pulled the blanket up over his head and hid.

"Damn you Willie, that's the third time tonight!"

One night there was a big party at the Officers' Club for some reason or no reason, but we were there. Colonel Willie Sonntag was talking to me, we each had drinks in our hands and we engaged a rather short, pretty lady in conversation when Willie dropped his glass full of booze right at the lady's foot. Of course it splashed up her legs and she roared at the Colonel, "Damn you, Willie, that's the third time tonight you did that!" I left.

Motormouth Crew-members during ORI

During the interrogation of crews by the Wing Commander and his staff regarding the portion of the Emergency War Order they were responsible for, many people felt compelled to show how much they knew, which led to getting in hot water over things they *didn't* know... They were finally able to just answer the question. This led to some consternation on the interrogators part, because they had to drag every answer out of each crew-member.

Reilly O. Godfrey—a legend

When I was stationed at Griffiss AFB I read a newspaper account of an Air Force Tanker (KC97) that had caught fire over Glens Falls, New York, and that the pilot, Captain Reilly O. Godfrey, had bailed his crew out and then bailed himself out near Glens Falls. The Tanker then proceeded to fly on to the Atlantic and out of radar coverage. Where it went down was not known at that time. Godfrey was an instructor at Goodfellow when I was a flight commander there. It was customary for instructors to take students on extended cross-country training flights over weekends. Godfrey was headed for Seattle one Friday night, stopped at Cheyenne, Wyoming, to refuel and then plotted a course direct to Rock Springs. He leveled at 10,000 feet and en route hit a tree on the side of a mountain. He climbed some and continued to Seattle. The airplane was Class 26 (non reparable) on arrival. Reilly discontinued instructing students and became a test pilot for maintenance at the request of the training group commander.

"We're sending you to Wright Patterson for Surgery"

I had just had my annual physical, which took up much of the day and when I arrived home I had a message to call the hospital. The doctor said I was to check into the hospital right away, as I had a spot on my lung and they were going to send me to Wright Patterson AFB for exploratory surgery. They said that my X-rays from last year showed the same thing. I tried to tell them that they did not have X-rays from last year since hospitals did not forward X-rays when you transferred. They didn't listen. I told them I had a mission to fly and would not put the squadron in such a bind. They said I would have to check in by Monday. I checked in Monday and waited and waited for someone to tell me more. Since they wouldn't listen to me I just had to wait. On Wednesday morning, a Dr. Sipple came into my room and said he had some news. My lung was fine, they had mixed me up with my Electronics Warfare Officer. They pushed me out the back door without even checking me out because I was irate. The EWO knew his condition and wasn't about to have surgery.

You sure get shook up on check rides

The SAC Combat Evaluation Group (GEG) at Barksdale AFB, Louisiana, conducted impartial evaluations of combat crews and had the guts to wear white flight caps. They terrorized wing commanders because they pulled no punches. I was promised that if I did a creditable job on a check ride with them, I would be upgraded to Instructor Pilot status. These missions were long and tiring, so that when we were on a bomb run on Watertown, NY, I told the co-pilot that I was going to close my eyes until the pre-ip and if I was asleep, wake me. He had to wake me and we went in to make a good bomb run. Then we had to go through a two-hour instrument check ride for me. I did fine and the evaluator made the comment in the debriefing that it looked like I really got shook up on check rides and just went on to sleep. He approved of my procedures, though, mentioning that I had coordinated with the crew before dozing off.

"Clawson, stand at Attention"

The Squadron Commander awarded me a good conduct medal

for WWII. If they only knew. (See Chapter IX, Major Bob Collins.)

Griffiss AFB was the only place that our family had lived on base until then. We all really wanted to leave Rome, NY as soon as possible. After my successful ride with CEG I was upgraded to Instructor status and sent to instructor school at Castle AFB, California. While there I received a call in the BOQ from my wife just as I was leaving to go fly. My navigator had called her and said there was an instructor slot at Castle. He knew I would like to take it. I hung up and called Willie and told him I wanted the slot at Castle, he wanted to know how the hell I knew about it since it had just been announced. I told him, and he said I had it.

Willie had asked a major if he would like the assignment before I called him and he said he would go home and discuss it with his wife. He came back and said he would take it. Willie told him Clawson already has it. The major knew I was in California and could not figure how I had beat him out of it. So we went to California and off alert.

Fig.21 'If you can't dazzle them with brilliance....'

Fig.22   Author prior to retirement

Chapter V: B-52 Operational Bomb Wing

329TH BOMBARDMENT SQUADRON
93RD BOMBARDMENT WING (H)
CASTLE AFB, MERCED, CA
MAY 1963—SEPTEMBER 1965

An assignment to Castle was considered a real plum in SAC. It was a training wing and had only a secondary role in the Emergency War Order (EWO). The best thing about it was that we didn't pull ground alert. All of our sorties were generated after declaring a high state of alert. Many of our students had previously flown B-47s and most were very competent in refueling and navigation, both high and low level. Three new crew-members had to be trained though from scratch: the Electronics Warfare Officer (EWO), navigator (since the navigator from B-47s became the radar navigator) and the gunner, who was enlisted status. We generally got these crews in the summer months and the new co-pilot trainees in the winter with the fog.

What the hell happened? Air brakes six under Tanker

On a routine training mission where all three of the pilot students were training to be co-pilots we were refueling with a KC-135 and the co-pilot student was not following my instructions and ended up too far forward, necessitating a simulated breakaway. I reached up under his hands and retracted the throttles sharply. My glove cuff caught the air brake handle and pulled it all of the way back to the number 6 position. This caused the airplane to nose up sharply and fall behind the Tanker very rapidly. When we were about a mile behind the Tanker we were still wondering what the hell had happened. A ride-along staff Lt. Col. pointed down to the airbrake handle. This could have been disastrous especially if it had occurred at night.

"I didn't have time to transition to Instruments"

My three co-pilot students were along the night we had to divert to Mather AFB near Sacramento, California due to heavy fog at Castle. The next morning Mather was 200 and 1/2 most of the morning, occasionally dropping below minimums. We taxied to the runway and when weather gave us minimums (200 1/2) we were ready to go. The airplane was an older B model with the gear lever on the far right side. The student had requested that he be allowed to make the take-off and I agreed. On take-off I had to reach across the cockpit to raise the gear and when I did my eyes left the instruments for a second. When I straightened up I saw we were 10 degrees nose down on the attitude indicator and headed straight toward the runway in front of us. We were 10 degrees nose down and below 200 feet with the gear up. I carefully started pulling back on the controls and we went back into the clouds and I flew the airplane up to 30,000 feet, put it on autopilot and started yelling at the student. He said he hadn't had time to transition to instruments. He had taken off on instruments and nearly crashed almost immediately after take-off.

No ass-chewing contest

Lt. Col Harold Ludlow was our squadron commander, and very much a gentlemen. He was "counseling" two Lt. Colonels and myself regarding the performance of our students from the past class of B-52 trainees. The LC's students had not done well and we were catching hell. My students, all co-pilots had done well on their check rides and I took great exception to be chewed out. Ludlow interrupted me with, "Don, this is no ass-chewing contest, I know who you worked for before [Willie Sonntag, at Griffiss AFB] but we are just having a conversation here."

Push the yoke forward

An instructor coming from a bomb wing to Castle to be an instructor pilot had several things to learn quickly. On landing for a touch and go (which were not allowed in the bomb wings) the pilot not flying was to reset the elevator trim tabs for the take-off. If the landing pilot held the yoke back too far, which he usually did, it cut out the trim switch. So on landing roll the first time this happened to me I had no idea what the problem was when I could not move the trim tabs.

How to handle a Lt. Col's kid when you are a Captain

A Lt. Col. from the Division Staff at Castle lived down the street from us in Merced, California. His son was an only child and spoiled by his mama. One night I looked out the front window of our house and saw him throwing eggs at our house and hitting the shutter around the front bedroom window. I told my sons, Charlie and Kevin, to get out there and clean up the mess the next day. They objected that they had not caused the mess. I said if you clean that up, I'll bet you will make sure that it doesn't happen again. I was right, they cleaned it up and then went down there and beat the hell out of that kid. No more trouble.

What are you going to do now?

On a rare crew practice sortie I was flying under a hood in the left seat on a day low-level mission through the mountains in western Nevada using the terrain avoidance radar when the co-pilot, who was the lookout, called on the inter-phone and asked me what I was going to do soon, I said nothing and pointed to the radar screen which indicated a mountain peak at about 2 o'clock. He removed the hood and the mountain was dead ahead of us. That ended my reliance on that damned radar! The radio altimeter was out also. We only had them a few weeks when a safety of flight bulletin put an end to its use except in day VFR weather.

I'm sure glad I get to see you operate

My two sons, Charlie and Kevin, and I went fishing at Lake Don Pedro and environs whenever we could. We had an old boat that my father-in-law had made and we went to Don Pedro one time towing the boat with an old Dodge sedan. This old man had some metal on the beach that he called a launching ramp and he charged a dollar for launching. We searched the car and everywhere we could think of to find a dollar. We could only find 99 cents, but the old man would not let us launch. He said "This is no cut-rate deal" and insisted that we wouldn't come all this way with no money. Some way we launched and fished. On the way home we had to take a detour around a washout and when we did I cut it too short and the right wheel on the boat trailer was off the road. We got out to assess our problem and Kevin and I were seriously trying to work something out. Charlie was standing with his arms crossed and doing nothing to help. He stated, "Boy, Dad, I'm sure glad I get to see how you operate! Now my kids won't think I'm so stupid."

My personal experience with trade school graduates (service academies) was not very positive. One of the navigators we had on the B-52 crew at Griffiss AFB was outstanding and did not rely on his ring-knocking buddies to get him out of trouble. Most of the others I knew well enough to make a judgment fell short of a full deck. One West Point captain that I felt was far short of an outstanding officer had the report I rendered removed from his file because it did not reflect what his service had been until then. I read his OER file at 8th Air Force and the endorsements from other West Pointers said he was the epitome of the grand graduate of that school. He had us on 180 and 360 degree headings going from Boston to Spain every time we crossed the pond with him. When the new school in Colorado started producing graduates we had the same type of attitude, as exemplified in the following anecdote.

This is not the proper learning situation

About 0200 we were at Beale AFB, north of Sacramento, shooting actual weather GCAs down to about 200-300 foot ceiling and making a touch and go landing and going around for another GCA. One Air Force Academy student co-pilot couldn't fly for shit and I was giving him hell. He came up with this classic, "This is not the proper learning situation." I threw him out of the seat and got another one of the students in the seat. I didn't hear anything like that from him and we completed the mission, giving the third one some actual experience in making GCAs.

Some of the older crews from the B-47 force used to take exception to my requirement that they pass a short test I put together on SAC Regulations. The only purpose of this little exercise was to convince them that they needed to know the rules. If you followed all the rules minutely you could never accomplish all of the training requirements in the training quarter to stay combat ready. If you talked too much about what you did to accomplish all of the training, you were in deep water.

Pass the test or don't graduate

I required all of my students at Castle study SAC Regulations and then take a test. It was necessary to know when they had broken a SAC Regulation, everyone did, but many of the crew-members I knew did not know the rules and therefore got in trouble by talking too much.

Oakland Center (ATC): "Looks like a Flock of Geese"

Large-scale missions required a liaison officer at the Center to provide technical information on the mission and the aircraft. The large-scale missions usually commenced with a Minimum Interval Take-Off (MITO). The MITO required a maximum separation on take-off of 15 seconds. With 10 or more B-52's taking off with less than 15 seconds interval the military had to assume responsibility for their own separation (MARSA). When the aircraft broke into radar coverage, the Controllers said it looked like a flock of geese.

Are you sure you're in a B-52 and not a B-25?

We flew a B-52 from Edwards AFB to Castle AFB with the flaps in an intermediate position because of a malfunction in the flap system, requiring that we not exceed 195 knots. Oakland Center had trouble believing we were a B-52 because of our altitude (we had filed a flight plan asking for 10,000') and airspeed, and queried us several times to confirm that we were indeed a B-52 and not a B-25.

If the Soviet Union had anywhere the amount of difficulty with their Air Defense force that the US did, we would have little or no trouble penetrating the defenses to hit our targets. Time and again we flew training missions against the ADC Nike force and seldom were even acquired, let alone tracked, to the point that we would have been hit. The following was an example of this ineptness. One of the reasons the Soviet TU 16 Badger bomber was not considered a threat was that we had no capability to realistically counter the threat. The excuse that they were not capable of a round trip to the US and back to the Soviet Union was pure hogwash. Some of our targets, especially in the B-47, required a bail-out as soon as we cleared the burst of our last weapon.

B-52 over Frankie's Joint (Lake Tahoe)

We were on a day training mission with students. We had a scheduled RBS run against Nike sites in the San Francisco area, so had to establish a "Track Number" with Air Defense Command (ADC). We were over Lake Tahoe on a very clear day at 27,000 feet. ADC requested we squawk a specific code on our IFF for identification. We did several times in response to their requests. They insisted that we were not over Lake Tahoe and thought we were spoofing them. We responded that we could see Frankie's Joint (referring to Frank Sinatra's Casino) and requested clearance for an RBS run. They were unable to acquire us on radar and we had to proceed and contact another control.

I think we have a good idea where we are

On a student night low-level mission in southern Oregon, when asked by the IP if they had a good position, the answer left a lot to be desired, so I set climb power and climbed out. The Instructor Navigator was pissed off because it ended that portion of the training for the navigator that night, but he had offered no re-assurance when student didn't sound sure of himself. When it came to flying in canyons in the middle of the night, not sure of the position of the aircraft, I drew the line.

B-52 Instructor hat inspection

Our squadron commander, Lt. Col. Harold Ludlow, tried to catch a couple of instructors that he knew did not even own garrison caps. The entire squadron was supposed to fall in for inspection. Of course a number of people were flying or off duty. One of the two he was trying to catch hid in the squadron latrine and Ludlow never caught him.

Appointed Defense Counsel in Airman Demotion case

My first experience as a party to board actions in the Air Force came when I was designated as defense counsel for a sergeant being considered for demotion. These assignments were never given to crew-members subject to alert. At Castle we were not on alert, and only when a build-up of forces was called for were we put in that position.

The first thing I had to do was be briefed by the Judge Advocate Generals (JAG) office on the case and pick up the folder with the charges and allegations. When I did this the young

Fig.23   B/G Harry Cordes presenting Meritorious Service Medal to author

attorney in the JAG said I wouldn't have to do much on this one, because they had him pegged and he would be demoted. This infuriated me and I called him an SOB and said now I was going to get him out of his problem. It turned out that the charges and allegations had no merit. I interviewed everyone involved, including his Master Sergeant supervisor, who testified for him. He was a staff sergeant doing hydraulic mechanical work. He was in a category of intelligence that was considered untrainable, or difficult to train at best. But he was trained and doing a good job. His family problems overwhelmed him and he was overreacting to them. The Deputy Commander for Maintenance (DCM) initiated the demotion procedures.

When we walked into the demotion board hearing, the president of the board was an EWO I was with at Griffiss AFB, and he didn't know I was assigned to Castle and gave me a loud greeting and we talked to a few minutes before the hearing began. I successfully countered each charge and allegation, and the board unanimously denied the demotion. The DCM was furious with me, but could not do anything to me for doing my job.

The maintenance squadron continued harassing the staff sergeant, however, and he would call me to help him. He was transferred to another base and I lost track of him.

Monday morning take-off, See you Friday, maybe

After almost three years of flying out of Rome, NY with all of its bad weather, I never diverted due to weather until I reported to Castle. During the winter we were usually given co-pilots to train and the fog was on the ground most of the time. The fog was so bad that one morning, a B-52 wing tip hit the Weather Observers' vehicle that was deployed near the runway, and they never saw it. We were allowed to take-off with the lowest minimums available for landing at Castle. The lowest minimums for the Navy was 100' ceiling and 1/4 mile visibility, therefore that's all we needed to take-off with three co-pilot trainees. This meant lots of extra training in the simulator on handling loss of electrical power, because that control panel was on the co-pilot side of the aircraft. We would always bring extra clothing for Monday morning take-offs because the fog to so bad that we usually ended up at

Edwards AFB on the desert and flew training missions out of there and returned Friday afternoon. There was usually a window of an hour or so when they tried to recover as many of the B-52s and KC-135s as they could.

B-52 disappears on Airbase

A night student-training mission was scheduled to include a three-ship Minimum Interval Take-off (MITO). This required a take-off interval of no more than 15 seconds, simulating a scramble departure of Alert force B-52s. We were the lead aircraft. The student aircraft commander and the student co-pilot were in their appropriate seats for start engines and taxi, The IP (me) was behind them trying to untangle interphone and radio cords, and when he looked up, the student aircraft commander had just inexplicably turned into a parking hardstand. Not having reverse thrust on the B-52, we had to shut the engines down, get a push back into the taxi lane and restart. In the meantime, the IP in the tower did not know all this, the second and third B-52 were taxiing and didn't know where the lead had disappeared. The IP (me) jumped into the co-pilot seat, restarted all eight engines in very short time, informed the tower and the other two B-52s held. We taxied around them in front of the tower, proceeded to the runway and made an on time take-off with an interval of less than 10 seconds. The IP in tower later told me that when he found out who the IP in the lead B-52 was he was rolling around on the tower floor laughing.

Shut down your Engines

A late Friday afternoon student sortie was in progress. We had just finished starting all eight engines and were ready to taxi for take-off when the Command Post called us and told us to shut down our engines and return to the Squadron. We requested authentication and that threw them off some, then the controller said, "Challenge me." We did, they authenticated and we shut down. The students were released and I was told to proceed to Base Operations and file a flight plan for Tyndall AFB, Florida. I was further instructed that when five other crew-members showed up, we were to proceed to Tyndall AFB. No explanation. The last navigator to arrive was a Lt. Col. that had been to Happy

Hour for some time. He slept all the way to Florida and wasn't sure how he had got there when we arrived.

Iron Bomb Tests

For the next week in Florida we engaged in the most bizarre missions I ever flew while in the Air Force. Live 750-pound iron bombs were loaded on B-52s in areas that were not cleared for live weapons handling. Damage was done to a B-52's outrigger gear that was never reported, although direct communications were maintained with the Vice Commander of the Strategic Air Command in Omaha. I drove with a Lt. Col., in a jeep, through the piney woods surrounding Tyndall looking for more 750 bombs for the tests. We found some and they were subsequently used to prove that the third bomb in the right aft rack still hit the bomb doors when dropped. They had determined this two years before and made no modifications. Why wouldn't the bomb still hit the door? I was later involved in some other bizarre missions with iron bombs, just to see what would happen…

Don't drop, intruder on range

The first bomb drops were scheduled for early Saturday morning. My crew was not scheduled to fly, but all crews were available and somewhat on standby. All B-52s and B-47s were loaded with weapons by that morning. The only scheduled flight was for a drop from 500' above the terrain on a land range used by Tyndall for live weapons training. Suddenly we were told we were to fly the mission. The primary B-52 had started taxi, hit an iron stanchion in the ramp and wiped out the right outrigger gear. We used a modified alert start, and were airborne shortly after being ordered to go. Due to low clouds and restricted visibility, we had trouble acquiring the target visually as well as with the radar, a requirement before dropping. The first run was aborted and we entered a racetrack pattern and came around again. A good run, everything go, when within 5 seconds to go, the control called on Guard Channel and ordered us to not drop. Afterwards we asked them what happened. Control told us there was an intruder on the range picking up scrap metal. The intruder must have thought it safe on a Saturday morning. Radar grabbed a handful of switches and luckily for the intruder, stopped the drop. Another racetrack pattern while the range was cleared and we were on the bomb run again. This time it was a normal drop until the bombs, twenty-seven 750-pound bombs, which had been salvoed, went off. Of course in retrospect we should have expected that we would be right over them when they exploded, but we all thought one or more had exploded in the bomb bay. It kicked the autopilot off and really shook us all up.

(The worst thing you could do in SAC was to scratch an airplane.)

Is that something the Crew should know?

On a subsequent test, we were instructed to drop on a radar reflector barge in the Gulf of Mexico at night. We questioned whether fishermen might be in the area. Answer—it's a restricted area and they should not be there. Our crew was termed a "5X" crew. It meant that we had never really trained together, and in our case everyone was an instructor in his specialty. I was a Captain and the co-pilot was a smart-ass Major. During the briefing for the mission, it was explained that the cameras installed in the bomb bay were working well. It also came out that the bombs were live bombs. A civilian Florida cracker, who had installed the cameras, crawling over the bombs to connect all the wires, was shocked to find out that he was crawling over "live bombs" and vowed never to do it again. While taxiing to take-off, we heard the Command Post controller talking to a Range Officer, and he said the B-52 was going to drop 29,000 feet south of the Radar Reflector Barge. *We had not been briefed to do this so the co-pilot quietly asked if that was something the crew should know.* We had intended to bomb the barge, which would have undoubtedly destroyed it. We then got a full briefing on the radio.

Request three hours in local area—Instrument Practice

After a week in Florida, and four or five sorties, we returned to Castle AFB late in the evening. Somewhat tired and bored, the co-pilot, the smart-assed one, and I decided to harass the rest of the crew. We switched to an unused UHF channel and broadcast a phony request for a three-hour extension of our mission in the local area for instrument practice. After the usual answer by me, "Stand-by," I granted the three-hour extension with the usual command post efficiency. The Nav's and the EW recognized both of our voices and said nothing, but the short black gunner riding in the tail did not and was seething. We really had forgotten about him. He later said he was going to throw out the cold beer we had stashed back there for after the flight.

Crack in Station 1655 Bulkhead

The B-52 was found to develop cracks in the 1655 Bulkhead and eventually the tail would fall off. This happened to staff crew over the Appalachians. The Butt pack (survival pack, attached to the parachute) had a sleeping bag in it and no one knew it. Maintenance had called me early in the morning to tell me that a crack had been found in the airplane I was scheduled to fly that evening and I would be cancelled. The only other Captain on the base that was a B-52 IP was scheduled to give a check ride to a Colonel from 15th Air Force, who had made arrangements with me to piggyback on my sortie and give the check. Since the Colonel was already on the base, they went on another airplane. The tail caught fire and they had to bail out. The entire crew got out all right, and the airplane crashed in the small town of Tranquility, in the San Joaquin Valley south of Merced.

I hope you get us Clearance to Land

We lost all electricals out over the ocean, and finally get some back, isolated. There was power to instruments on the pilot side and lights on the co-pilot side. 15th Air Force had put a hold on our landing. We got the gear down, flaps set and told Castle Command Post we were in penetration and hoped they could get clearance from 15th by the time we got to the end of the runway, because we were going to land. We landed, and on the roll out, Tower stated that the Fire Chief said our brakes were on fire. We stopped on the runway and evacuated the aircraft. The ride-along Tanker co-pilot in training, with no gratitude for the smooth way we handled the emergencies, said he would never ride with us again.

Training B-47 Pilots in B-52 crosswind landings

The technique for the approach and actual touchdown on the runway in the B-47 was significantly different than that used in the B-52. The B-47 was flown in a crab with some cross control to maintain the runway heading and then just as you were touching down the crab was removed to align the aircraft with the runway. The B-52 was equipped with rotatable gear so that it could be adjusted to be parallel with the runway and the aircraft remain in the crab. Many times you would touch down viewing the runway through the co-pilot's front windscreen. The problem with this in transition was to watch that the ex-B47 pilot didn't kick out the crab at the last minute. The instructor was usually alert for this especially after the first time the student was successful in removing the crab and landing with the gear cockeyed to the runway.

The Base Commander at Castle was somewhat unique in that usually the older Colonels were given this job, and about their only prerogative was to change the direction of the one-way streets. This caused a lot of grief at times. One Base Commander's greatest joy was to get the people who ran the train used on the base to let him run it.

SAC Division Commanders and their Staffs

The Division Commander (DC) located at Castle AFB had a small staff that truly had little or nothing to do. They all played par golf and enjoyed life. The Division Commander was a Napoleon type of guy who visited the Bank of America Branch on the base, which leased space in a WWII-type barracks building with water-stained windows. He demanded that the bank manager clean the windows. This was an impossibility, and when the DC revisited the bank and the windows were basically the way they were before he proceeded to break some of them. Why he was allowed to get away with this is unknown.

This was about the time in my life that I made all the dumb decisions I could in a matter of weeks. I had applied for BOOTSRAP at Fresno State to get a master's degree. The Wing Commander approved it and it went to SAC Headquarters where they turned me down because they said I didn't have enough retain ability. Someone had picked up on the fact I had enlisted when I was 17 years old and didn't notice that I was a regular officer with 12 years commission service, leaving at least 16 years retain ability. I didn't get on an airplane and go to Omaha like I should have. I re-applied the next year and the WC denied it because they were short of instructor pilots. The personnel people offered to put me in the simulator or command post so I would be sure of selection next time I applied. The problem I saw with this was every officer serving in these positions had either done something stupid while flying, like dropping a large fuel tank off the B-52 onto a chicken farm in the middle of the night, or could not qualify as an instructor. My squadron commander was on leave when I decided to resign and so I didn't have any counseling available.

Resignation from the Regular US Air Force

One of the most difficult periods in my life began with my voluntary resignation from the Regular Air Force to take a job with United Airlines in Denver, Colorado. I joined the Wyoming Air National Guard, and because of my training in the C-121 was able to volunteer for extended active duty and was accepted. The two years I was away from the Air Force were miserable. The next dumbest thing I did was not accepting my regular commission back when offered on Taiwan. Thinking UAL would terminate me if I did this, I rejected it—only to find that I could not get back to UAL in time to be reinstated anyway. Later on when I was working for Brigadier General Harry Cordes he told me that my worst enemy couldn't have done me in any better than I did myself.

Last Flight in a B-52

I never was sure whether the Wing had selected me to fly this mission because I was smart, or because if they lost the crew, I was going to be gone anyway.

We were assigned an old "B" model B-52 with one under-wing bomb rack with a load of 750-pound bombs on it. We went out to sea with a minimum crew and an engineering type on board to determine what would happen if a mission was flown with a mixed load of munitions. The scenario would have thermonuclear weapons in one bomb bay and iron bombs in the other bomb bay and on one rack on each wing, dropping the iron bombs first and then the nuclear weapons. The problem we were looking at was if the iron bombs were dropped, but one rack of bombs would not release and the rack could not be jettisoned. Subsequently the nuclear weapons would be dropped, requiring a post-strike maneuver using a maximum bank turn immediately after the drop of each weapon to put the tail of the aircraft to the burst. This type of turn increases the g-forces on the aircraft significantly. The people watching the rack and bombs said the movement of the rack was spectacular and they suggested that we not look at it.

I left Merced and went to work for United Airlines in the training center in Denver, Colorado. About the beginning of the second week I knew I had make the biggest mistake of my life going to work for a commercial airline.

Chapter VI: C-121 Transport Wing

Almost the first thing I did after checking in with United Airlines was to go to Cheyenne, Wyoming and join the Air National Guard. This unit flew C-121 (Constellation) aircraft with a tie to the Military Airlift Command. The Brigadier General commanding the unit was the local beer distributor and the unit was really run by sergeants. Military discipline was not what I had experienced in SAC so I was always halfway in trouble all the time.

MAC 34, you're lined up with wrong runway, pull up

Landing at Frankfurt, Germany one night in heavy fog, I was standing behind the pilots when the approach control instructed the crew to pull up swiftly because they had selected the wrong approach plate and were making the approach to the wrong parallel runway in minimum weather for the approach.

MAC 43, Wake Island advises you may have flat tire(s)

On final approach to Hickam AFB, Tower advised that Wake reported debris on runway after we left, which could be from a blown tire. They advised caution!

"Engine fall off airplane?"

A Flying Tigers C-121 radioed to Hong Kong Radio on HF that they had had a fire on the number 3 engine, they feathered it and it fell off the airplane. Hong Kong radio came right back with "Understand, number three engine unserviceable."

"No, that's not what I said," he replied and what he had said the first time. This time Hong Kong radio operator comes back with "Engine fall off airplane"?

Beer Distributor as Wing Commander

The Air National Guard unit at Cheyenne, Wyoming, was a good old boy unit, where Master Sergeants were in charge. The Wing Commander's motto was, "The unit has Hallmark Crews". Lots of military discipline had been forgotten, as the enlisted personnel always accompanied the officers' to the officers clubs, especially when overseas.

"Standby for possible go-around"

One trip from Guam to Wake Island was made in miserable weather all the way. It ended with me flying and on final approach to Wake being told that an aircraft was on the runway taxiing for the pad at the end of the runway and I might have to go around. There were not parallel taxi-ways on Wake at that time. The crosswind was so bad I had full throw of the yoke and all the rudder I could get to stay lined up with the runway. We did not have to go around and when I landed I had to have the co-pilot retract the throttles because I could not let go of the yoke.

Air National Guard hauling scrap lumber

One trip I flew as a crew-member on a C-121 from Cheyenne, Wyoming, to McChord AFB in Washington State, to Cubi Point Naval Air Station in the Philippines. From there we were to fly cargo to Da Nang, Vietnam. We were given a cursory load of the rottenest looking lumber, all split and bent, to haul into the battle zone. We all felt as if there must be more to war supplies than that.

What happened to the sandbag revetments?

On the first two or three trips to Da Nang, we noticed that several large sandbag revetments were built right outside the door at Base Operations. We commented on them to the base ops personnel, and they confirmed that they had come in handy more than once. The last time we were there the revetments were all gone and a nice lawn was starting to grow in their place. The master sergeant weather forecaster told us that the Base Beautification Officer had come by and said the revetments looked like hell and then proceeded to remove them.

All Civilians are Dismissed

There was a daily briefing for all flight crews flying into Vietnam, military and civilians. The Cubi Point operations personnel would brief any en route problems and weather forecaster would guess at what the weather would be on arrival and any other pertinent facts about the route. Then the civilian pilots were required to leave and the military would receive a classified briefing. In late 1964 Hawk surface to air missiles were installed at Tan Son Nhut, Bien Hoa, Cam Ranh Bay and Da Nang airfields, manned by US Army defense command troops. In the event of an attack on any of these bases, the Army would go into free fire and shoot at anything flying. The codeword to do a 180-degree turn and leave the area was classified, and so was not given to the civilian airline pilots hauling military cargo and personnel into Vietnam.

On the C-121 aircraft operated by the National Guard there was a large oven just inside and opposite the rear loading door. The crews used it to heat frozen dinners and such things.

"Who was the dumb bastard that put the beans in the oven?"

I bought some Campbells baked beans for the trip, why I don't know. Out of Cubi Point in the Philippines en route to Da Nang in Vietnam I put the beans in the oven to warm up. I forgot them and also forgot to vent the can. Now for most of us on the airplane this was our first trip to the war zone. Our loadmaster was a guy about 6'3" and 250 lbs. He was sitting in the passenger seat directly across the aisle from the oven when the beans exploded, blew the door open and sprayed hot beans all over the side of him and the airplane opposite the oven. The "beaned" loadmaster was ready to kill the dumb bastard who put the beans in the oven. I was cleaning the airplane all the way back to Cheyenne.

Eventually I made five trips to Vietnam with the Guard unit along with two trips to Germany. I didn't fit in with the way things were done in the civilian sector and was extremely happy when I was accepted for extended active duty again.

My Dad was never a great fan of my choice of careers and so when I told him I was going back on active duty his response was "You got out without getting killed, and they are going to send you to Vietnam—are you nuts?"

Chapter VII: Active duty again!

EC-121 Air Defense Wing
964th Airborne Early Warning &
Control Squadron (ADC)
McClellan AFB, North Highland, CA
December 1967—March 1969

The Air Defense unit at McClellan AFB had been there for many years and had received their airplanes when new. There were two basic missions. One was to fly the radar platform with a large contingent of Combat Information Center (CIC) personnel, including weapons controllers, on an almost continuous forward extension of the Early Warning Radar out over the Pacific Ocean to warn of possible flights of heavy Soviet bombers approaching the Continental United States (CONUS). The other task on the EW mission that they were required to do was log all commercial and other airborne traffic approaching the US. The peacetime traffic would have an operational radar beacon on the aircraft, making it easy to identify them. Any foreign bomber approaching certainly would not be "squawking". The radar operators did not want to miss an airline plane because these were on the Air Defense Command schedule and could be checked against the logs, so the operators would fly with the radar set on beacon to be sure. The raw radar that would be necessary to detect a foreign bomber would not be available. The aircraft commanders would from time to time try to monitor this, but the Chief of the CIC would fuss that the a/c was interfering with his operation. It was obvious that not many people took this mission very seriously.

The other mission was to support the College Eye task force in Southeast Asia. A rear echelon maintenance base was established on Taiwan and the crews would rotate between Korat, Thailand and Tainin AB on Taiwan We would fly missions out of Korat exercising positive control on all US fighters north of the Mekong in Laos and Mig Watch in the Gulf of Tonkin.

Long-tenured full Colonel—Wing Commander with plushed C-121

The Wing Commander was one of the top-ranking full colonels

in the Air Force. He was not respected by the Wing personnel. He had coerced Air Asia, a maintenance firm on Taiwan, into plushing up this C-121. When it was used for flight training, the crew chief told us we were to wear booties to cover our dirty flight boots. Being me, I would not comply, but no one made an issue of it. Higher headquarters found out about the airplane, it disappeared and damned if he didn't have another one done up.

Bolt of lightning hit long wire

We were ferrying an EC121 to Florida for major maintenance. Over Jackson, Mississippi, we were flying near a large storm. I had my head in the radar scope and had just told the pilot that if he turned a few degrees to the starboard we should miss the heavy part of the storm, when just then lightning hit the long HF antenna that ran from the top of one of the tails to just above the cockpit. It broke the wire, making a hell of a lot of noise slapping the fuselage and energy came into the cockpit and caused the HF set to burn out and cause a lot of smoke in the cockpit. The first engineer, an old guy, was shaving in the latrine at the back of the airplane and it about scared him to death.

"All that trouble for nothing"—Gear Collapses

I was one of two aircraft commander (AC) candidates getting check rides one day in the EC 121, and for some reason or none we each had our own check pilot (IP) on board. The first A/C went through his check and the IP would put the gear handle in an intermediate position after the pilot had called for it to be lowered and checked it down and safe to land. He did this several times and then my IP did the same thing with me. This was causing stress on the mechanism. The purpose the IP had in mind was to be sure the pilot would call for a recheck of the gear as we approached the landing point. Both of the A/Cs did this several times. On the last approach from which we were going to land, my IP was satisfied with the check and the gear was lowered and checked and the damned thing was unsafe. I gave him hell, saying we'd done this enough already; he said it was for real. Both the other A/C and I refused to participate in the recovery of the aircraft, since the IPs had broken it. We then flew around, dumped fuel, had a chase plane check the gear, flew by the tower, had them check it and got ready to land. We landed, rolled out, stopped and had the ground crew insert the safety pins and were waved on by ground crew to taxi. We heard a heavy thumping on the airplane right below our seats. We stopped immediately and it turned out that the crew-member inserting the pins in the gear was on the nose wheel strut! He left shaking his fist at us.

We had pulled the ropes loose that were for emergency escape from the airplane on the ground and opened several of the windows in case we couldn't open the back door. We taxied to the parking area and the engineer made the remark that we went to all that trouble and nothing happened. But, when the engines were winding down, the hydraulic pressure that was holding the gear in position bled off and the right main gear inexplicably collapsed. We were thrown around in the airplane quite a bit. The back door was then opened and we started to use the ropes, but the ground was right there and we jumped and ran like hell. The EC-121 had integral fuel tanks in the wings and we figured that most of the contents were fumes, making it a highly dangerous piece of equipment. The young engineer, who was right behind me said afterwards he wondered how an old fat guy like me could run so fast… I was confident that the airplane was going to blow. It didn't. It was subsequently found that the part resting against the manual pin inserted by the ground crew, which would prevent the gear from collapsing, was broken—evidentially, by all of the manipulation—and the ground crew was cleared of any misdeed.

"Colonel, we don't allow Observers, you're number one

I don't know where all the old colonels came from in this ADC Wing but one staff full colonel decided he would have a boondoggle and got put on orders to go to water survival school at Perrin AFB in Texas that all of the crew-members were required to attend. Because most of our missions were flown over water it was considered essential for survival if we either had to ditch the airplane or bail-out. At the first briefing this older Chief Master Sergeant who was in charge of the school started assigning numbers to each member of the class to determine in what order we were to accomplish the training—such as being blown across a field by a big fan while we were wearing an open parachute on the ground, or jumping off the tall tower while strapped in a parachute harness and attached to a cable that went to the ground. Seniority was prime for numbering. The colonel could see this coming and informed the sergeant that he was just an observer. The sergeant came right back with, "We don't have observers in this school, Colonel, that makes you number one." He had do everything first and some of it was spooky.

Chief Master Sergeant removed inflation bottle and plug

We had a really outspoken and crusty senior master sergeant as first engineer on our crew and he had argued with the Chief running the school a couple of times about something being stupid. When it came time to roll off a pontoon boat in the middle of the night with an un-inflated, life raft under our arm and life jacket un-inflated our sergeant was there. Once we were in the water the first thing we did was get the life jacket inflated and then work on the boat. All of the boats had CO_2 bottles with a cord to release the gas, which inflated the boat. Once in the boat we were to fire several flares from our Very pistol and paddle to an island that had a bonfire burning. The Chief had removed the CO_2 from the bottle for the senior sergeant, requiring him to inflate it with his own wind. The plug to hold the hot air in was also removed. The senior sergeant was fit to be tied by the time he reached the island but kept his mouth shut for a little while after that.

Second gear problem—SOP called for fire truck under wing

After the first gear problem, maintenance obtained some strut locks that would go around the extended strut, preventing collapse. We had a similar indication later on one of my crew's missions. We went through same procedures only this time we informed the tower that the published standard operating procedures (SOP) for this emergency was to land on the runway, set the brakes and keep the engines running at more than idle. Once we'd stopped, the fire chief was to place one of his fire trucks under the wing to prevent the airplane from collapsing on the ground. The tower of course told us to stand by and they contacted the fire chief. He said he didn't care what the SOP called for, he sure as hell was not going to put one of his trucks under our wing.

We landed, had the pins put in the gear, taxied to the parking area and maintenance told us to shut down. The strut locks had been locked up in quality control and no one had the key. We refused to shut the engines down until all of our crew was off and clear of the aircraft and then the maintenance crew shut down without incident.

Missiles Inbound Exercise

The wing was to participate in a large-scale exercise that had all 45 airplanes and ground power equipment attached and all crews on board the airplanes. The airplanes had a radar platform that took some time to erect and be safe to taxi. It also took a long time after shutdown before they could start again. The crews were instructed to start engines, which was accomplished.

They stood by for some time and then the command post broadcast a code word. No one in the airplanes knew what the code word meant. The code word had been changed a year or so before after many years, but the crews had not been briefed on the change. The instruction in code was to taxi and simulate take-off as soon as possible, because an intercontinental missile was confirmed to be inbound. By this time some crews had shut down, and the crews were wandering around the ramp. After my years in SAC where everyone was on top of alert and execution procedures, I was amazed, and said so. I was made the new training officer, responsible for instructing the crews on emergency war order procedures.

COLLEGE EYE DEPLOYMENT

While deployed to Southeast Asia in support of College Eye we were assigned to the 6214th Support Squadron (Taiwan). The support base was located at Tainan City in the southern part of Taiwan. While TDY we would spend eight days at Tainan City and two weeks at Korat, flying quite frequently. There was a limitation on the number of people allowed in Thailand at any one time, so we were required to rotate with other crews.

College Eye

I had been recalled to active duty from the Wyoming Air National Guard where we flew C-121's. The Air Force had almost exhausted the supply of people who had ever flown them. Obviously that was the motivation for recalling me. The unit at McClellan had a standing requirement for replacements for the TDY duty at Korat and so when I arrived the two lieutenant colonels next up to go saw their salvation in me. They scheduled me for ground school, simulator and flying training all together. I worked hard to finish just to show them I could do it. I got even later when they were both assigned to my Igloo White squadron at Korat, where I was Chief of Stan Eval, and they had to pass my evaluation of their flying abilities.

> It was not hard to leave McClellan AFB; the ADC element I was in was not where the Air Force put the best of the best. Most of the people had been there so long and the mission was not actually doing anything. The people just went through the motions and the senior officers were not very involved in the mission. Even the TDY mission in Southeast Asia was redundant to other services missions. There were so many airplanes over the Gulf of Tonkin, it was dangerous just trying to stay out of each other's way.

Chapter VIII: EC-121R Reconnaissance Wing

Korat Royal Thai Air Base was located near the center of Thailand with a small number of Thai aircraft and personnel. It was home to two USAF fighter wings, however, and the units of C-121 aircraft. The fighters were F105s (Wild Weasels) and F-4's. The C-121 units were flying two different missions. One was supported with TDY aircraft from the AEW&C squadrons at McClellan AFB, California and was limited to a headcount in country. They were known by the project name of College Eye. The other unit of C121s consisted of two reconnaissance squadrons and were supporting project Igloo White and had the call sign "Bat Cat". College Eye was a JCS directed mission that provided MIG watch in the Gulf of Tonkin and positive control over all fighter actions north of the Mekong River in Laos. I had one tour in each of the C-121 units. This chapter will be divided into the two missions.

COLLEGE EYE DEPLOYMENT (FORWARD BASE)

The tour with College Eye was actually very enjoyable except for the realization of what we were doing to Vietnam on the ground. A couple of trips down the Ah Shau valley was enough to make you sick. We spent two weeks at Korat flying every other day, but never more than two days off. Because of the limitations on the number of US personnel in the country, we had then to fly back to Tainan City on Taiwan. We stayed in a Chinese hotel in the downtown area with only one day of duty, in case the maintenance people wanted a test flight after maintenance. The rest of the time we were pretty free to do what we wished.

"I'm 090 degrees, 30 miles Channel 72"

That was what I heard upon crossing into Laos from the Da Nang area for the first trip to Korat, Thailand, from Taiwan. A fast mover (jet) had been hit by anti-aircraft fire and said he was bailing out, that he was on the 090 degree radial at 30 miles from

Channel 72 (which was a clandestine VORTAC station in Laos). Within five minutes he was on the ground with his radio active, FAC-ing for the protective fighters trying to keep the bad guys away from him until the Air America helicopters could reach him to bring him out. The guy was so calm, it sounded like he did that every morning before breakfast.

Oil Pressure zero on Number 3—feathered

The ride-along IP raised hell with the engineer for feathering an engine because the oil pressure gauge had just gone directly to zero, before telling the pilot. The Engineer bet the IP that because of what he had done there was little or no damage to the engine. Engineer won the bet.

Time in the Saddle Doesn't Matter—if You're Stupid

This is what I was telling the First Engineer for his resisting my order to set power to climb, and he was telling me how long he had been flying in the airplane. Just then the young second engineer, who was coming through curtains, heard this and beat it, telling the crew that those old guys are fighting like hell and he wasn't about to go up there. I was one of the older crew-members in the Wing and the first engineer on our crew was definitely the oldest flight engineer in the Wing.

"You did not see a fighter cross the Laos-Chinese border northbound"

The Combat Information Center (CIC) officer in the back of our aircraft reported that a fighter they were tracking was rapidly approaching the Laos-Chinese border and they had broadcast the code word requiring the fighter to reverse course and steer clear of the border. The CIC reported that when the word went out the fighter was at the border and his IFF went silent. Thirty minutes later they picked up the IFF right at the border and the fighter must have been in afterburner because he was really leaving China in a hurry. The incident was reported by CIC to the intelligence debriefer. The next day the CIC was told that he did not see any fighter enter China and he was not to discuss it further.

Aussie ground forward air controller—Northern Laos

On long night orbits we used to listen on tactical frequencies for some excitement. Several times we heard this distinctly Aussie voice from a ground forward air controller. He was working with a Laotian major on his link. Black B-26s came out of Nakhon Phanom in northeastern Thailand and would have this Aussie talk them into targets. One night he was disgusted with the bombers because they could not locate the target he was describing, so he said he would shoot a Very pistol shell into the area. The range of a Very pistol is so short it astounded everyone that he would do that. He finally said he would have to leave as he could hear the bad guys. He had previously asked the bombers if they had seen the village in their flare; they had, and he said, "Well, just drop on it." They asked him if that was the target and he said, "No mate, but it'll be good enough." Our guys said no thanks and took their bombs home that night.

US Navy claimed to have shot down a MIG

Our crew had been assigned MIG Watch in the Gulf of Tonkin and at the morning briefing the intelligence staff said that Navy jets from one of the carriers in the Gulf had shot down a MIG the day before. The Air Force soon put the damper on their exuberance by telling them that they had shot an unarmed drone recon. bird that had successfully avoided all the North Vietnamese anti-aircraft and completed its planned mission. Just as it arrived "feet wet", the Red Crown Destroyer detected it and alerted the carrier force and they launched. I met a Lt. Colonel at SAC Headquarters a year or so later who had been the controller of the drone and he said they called the Navy on Guard Channel and begged them not to shoot the drone down. I guess the adrenalin was running so high they never heard the repeated calls and zapped the drone. Within a day our wing staff was telling us that we were not to discuss it anymore. The Air Force and the Navy had reached a gentlemen's agreement not to discuss the matter further. I don't know what the Quid for the Quo, was but this is the unvarnished story.

You have all the missiles on Hainan Island ginned up—better scram

Trying to stay out of the way of all the other airplanes flying over the Gulf of Tonkin doing the same thing we were, we had taken up an east-west orbit which ended up too close to Hainan Island and this gave the Chinese reason to bring their missiles to high state of alert. The *Red Crown* destroyer up near Haiphong Harbor called us and said we had caused the missiles to start peaking their power and that it would be a good idea if we left the area quickly. We did.

Don't fly over Tiger Island

We were frequently cautioned in the mission briefing before going out to the Gulf of Tonkin for MIG watch not to fly over Tiger Island, because the Vietnamese had guns on it and would shoot at us. Tiger Island was just off the coast at the DMZ. Naturally, some aircraft commander doubted the presence of guns and flew over it on the way home one day and got a big hole in the airplane, blew up a crew-members boots next to the bunk he was resting in, and really pissed the crew off at him. No one would fly with him after that. They sent him home early.

Later we heard that the battleship *Iowa* had done at least one thing of significance: they leveled Tiger Island to the waterline.

IGLOO WHITE

While I was TDY to College Eye I received orders for permanent change of stations to Korat in the Igloo White program. I went home and moved my family out of base quarters to the only place my wife said she could find, on the seventh hole of the Rocklin Golf course. Since this was a permanent change I had to go through the jungle survival school at Clark AB in the Philippines. Eventually we arrived at Korat again. New arrivals at Korat usually had to wait for a while to get air-conditioned hootches. I simply found an empty bed in the College Eye area and moved in there. Eventually we were all assigned newer quarters. According to one author, Igloo White, "despite the expenditure of enormous effort and billions of dollars, proved to be a spectacular failure for a variety of reasons, the most important being it was totally the wrong system for existing conditions".

The Igloo White mission involved dropping sensors in areas along the Ho Chi Min Trail in such a way that the movement of personnel and equipment could be detected and tracked. A large computer complex in Thailand was to receive signals from the airplanes flying over the sensors and analyze them and send a message to Seventh Air Force in Saigon and the planners would produce fragmentary (frag) orders for fighters to hit the targets the next day. Timeliness was a problem. The EC 121 carried a full complement of people in the Combat Information Center who had the capability of plotting the activations and calling the C 130 Airborne Command and Control Center in our area, and could give specific coordinates on parked trucks so that they could be bombed immediately. This was not allowed because the General at the computer center said this circumvented the system. One of our aircraft commanders had a long history of working for the CIA and DIA said that we just didn't understand the mission, we were to count the trucks, not kill them.

It was evident our system worked so badly that the North Vietnamese knew what we were doing but realized that we were not effective in stopping the flow of material. They fired small caliber anti-aircraft ammunition at each of the orbiting aircraft most of the time we were on station, but unless we were to lose an engine and be forced to a lower altitude it was ineffective.

Had we effectively used the system that existed and stopped or impeded the flow of material, I am sure the North would have simply hauled 57mm radar-directed guns down the Trail and would have taken out each airplane on orbit in one night. As it was, though, the oil leaking from our engines didn't bother them too much.

Before 1968, someone in the 553 Recon Wing devised a wing emblem, which was displayed beside the bandstand in the Officers Club at Korat. It consisted of a life-size Edsel grille and a large plaque at the bottom with the wing designated on it that looked almost exactly like Figure 16. Of course, Robert McNamara was president of Ford Motor Company, and was key in developing the Edsel, and as Secretary of Defense he was the only reason for Igloo White. Both were miserable failures.

"We're going to war, load your pistols"

I climbed on board the EC 121 after the pre-flight was complete to administer a six-month standardization check flight. To my amazement all the enlisted and officer crew-members were loading their snub-nosed .38s. I went up to the cockpit and the aircraft commander (A/C) was loading his too. I instructed them to have all of them unloaded immediately. The Lt. Col. A/C argued with me, but complied. I told the Ops Officer about it and he immediately wanted to know which crew was involved. I did not tell him which crew. I told him to announce the policy regarding this and if he couldn't tell which crew it was then, I would tell him. Of course when he brought it up the A/C violently disagreed with him and I smiled at the Ops Officer and he knew who it was.

Some new Crew-members panicked first night on station (BAT CAT)

The orbits we were assigned were over or very near the Trail, so the North Vietnamese Army took measures to counter us. The amount of 37 mm anti-aircraft fire that came up was amazing, but it all fell short of our altitude. We could never figure out why they didn't bring some 57 mm guns down and knock all of us down in one night. It was quite a display, though, and for new troops it shook them for a while. You could look up and down the Trail and tell exactly where the other Bat Cat aircraft were. When the aircraft banked for turn it looked like the explosions were right outside your window.

Slap! "Wake up! That's for real!"

The Wing staff EW was flying in the EW slot on Bat Cat Mission and hadn't been able to raise me on interphone so he came forward and slapped me on the head and pointed to the radar detector on the instrument panel and said, "That's for real! Let's get the hell out of here, they're just about to fire a SAM at us."

When we returned to base, he found out that they had known of the SAM location right after we had left Korat, but for some reason failed to tell us. The EW officer really came unglued.

BAT CAT--0 AND BAT CAT---0 AT 0200

I flew with a crew for the purpose of giving a six-month check to a young co-pilot who normally worked in the command post but boasted even in the survival school at Clark that he was a much superior pilot to old guys like me, little did he think I would be Chief of Stan Eval. The crew was briefed that I would be checking the co-pilot, but that the rest of the crew-members were to be supporting him in the usual manner. I also took my turn at the controls while on station. On the approach into Korat at about 0300 we heard another aircraft in the area. Both aircraft call signs were Bat Cat, ours being 20 and the other 30. Approach control gave Bat Cat 30 vector, however our intrepid co-pilot only heard Bat Cat —0 and took the vector intended for the other aircraft. Approach control was right on the ball and caught it and corrected it. The co-pilot and pilot flunked the ride. The pilot had not backed him up and if it had been at Da Nang could have caused a catastrophe due to the hilly terrain. The pilot, a Lieutenant Colonel, was inflamed and never spoke to me again that I can remember. I immediately went to the training section and demanded that the call signs be changed in such a way that we would not have the possibility of a mix-up like that again.

Passenger pick-up 0300—Saigon

A new Colonel selectee at Korat had been to a meeting in Saigon and wanted the Bat Cat aircraft from the orbit west of the field to land and pick him up before returning to Korat. He could have waited another hour or so and come back on the Scat Back T-39, but insisted on our going in after him. Control said they would give us a GCA if we would accept vectors around friendly fire on final. We declined, made our own pattern inside the field perimeter, landed long, taxied like hell and threw a rope ladder out the back door, for the Colonel to get on the aircraft, keeping engines running. The Colonel declined our rope ladder and had the ground crew wheel the regular loading ramp to the aircraft, thus delaying us some. Even so we taxied out and took off in something less than ten minutes on the ground.

Wing Commander Ostendorf Stand Board Check

Colonel Ted Ostendorf had flown with me several times at McClellan where he was in charge of all 121 aircraft modifications in the Air Force. He knew that prior to my recall I had worked in Standards at the United Air Lines training center in Denver. He was the most nervous examinee I had while at Korat. When we returned the next morning, he elected a GCA for his instrument approach part of the check. After landing we had to hold up our taxi for another aircraft and I asked him what his minimums for the GCA were. He looked at me and said that he knew I was going to ask him and he didn't know. We went to breakfast together so I could debrief the ride and he asked me if that had happened to a United captain, would he have failed the ride? Of course he knew the answer, but since he would write his own corrective action, we simply took note of it.

"You Have to Unload All This Junk"

We were ferrying one of the oldest EC-121s in the inventory anywhere, from Korat to Lake City, Florida. Landing on Guam we came under the operational control of the Ferry Command. This big Lt. Col. told me I had permission for the passengers, but no freight, and I would have to unload all of the elephants, pachinko machines, bars, and a lot of other junk that people had put on the airplane to take to McClellan AFB. He also wanted us to take 24 hours on Guam so we wouldn't land in the middle of the night at Hickham AFB and make his people get up in the middle of the night to meet us. We started to have a bonnybrook, but then something was said about SAC and B47's and we were fast buddies from then on and he forgot about the "junk". We remained at Guam 24 hours in exchange for 24 in Honolulu, where my sister lived.

We found out later that one of the EC-121 Wing Commanders had been through there earlier and had given the Ferry Command Lt. Colonel a real bad time, so it was payback time. Luckily we found common ground and the whole trip turned out to be fun.

"What did you say?"—"I said drop"—"Okay"

We had been informed by a control center at Nakhon Phanom in North-east Thailand that we would have to move our orbit, near the Laos border to the south, as a Navy jet fighter was coming in from the water to make a drop in our area. The controller told the fighter he had radar contact and to be ready to drop on his count of three. He counted down, one, two, three, *drop*. The fighter pilot called him and asked what he had said, the controller said, "Drop". Fighter pilot said, "Okay." He was traveling close to the Mach so you can imagine he didn't come close and no one seemed to care.

Flight Surgeon—Non-combatant—no weapon

The flight surgeon assigned to our Squadron was a Captain and a good guy, if not a little naive. He insisted that he would only fly with me, because being Chief of Stand Board I was bound to know more than the average dog. He would not carry the snub-nose .38 we were issued because he claimed to be a non-combatant. I couldn't convince him that the Vietnamese couldn't tell that, and anyway the gun was signally for, shooting yourself or hunting something to eat, not for combating the NVA.

Explosive Ordinance Officer—Northern Laos Excursions

We became accustomed to a young Air Force Captain showing up every once in a while to fly with us to get his income tax exemption for combat zone duty. His regular duty was to infiltrate into Northern Laos with an Explosive Ordinance Sergeant, and they would carry explosives to blow bridges and disrupt life for the Pathet Lao soldiers. They would live off the land for up to a month before being extracted by air. Their presence in Laos was never acknowledged, therefore to get combat pay and tax exemption, he had to fly with us.

Wing Vice Commander, "Hit by lightning"

We had been on orbit for several hours, when the Vice Commander, an old fighter pilot, was in the cockpit and we had a large noise as the static electricity (St. Elmo's fire), which had built up on the nose and looked like a neon sign, discharged. It scared the hell out of the Colonel and he wanted me to write up the incident as a lightning strike… Had a hell of a time convincing him that it was just static electricity discharging.

Night Orbit over Muy Ba Din—"Fourth of July"

The bad guys had decided one day to take the top of Muy Ba Din, just to the west of Saigon, where our sensor readers were located, so they went up and killed the team and wrecked the equipment. Our EC-121s then had to orbit the area to read the sensor activations. As the sensors were activated, the combat control center in rear of our airplane called them in and artillery was directed to the area. B-52s were also active in the area and we could see bombs exploding almost under our nose, and the C-130 gunships were spraying what looked like a red hose into the mountain with a large floodlight on the target area. We would frequently be told to alter our orbit to avoid the artillery, which was going up through our altitude, and the B-52s dropping bombs creating an atmosphere that reminded us of the Fourth of July. We were everybody's target that night.

Do you really know how much fuel you have left?

I conducted a self-assigned, squadron-approved, study of procedures for calculating fuel reserves for maximum endurance flights in the EC-121. I started by collecting every flight engineer's log of each flight. Each refueling log was checked to determine how much fuel was put on the aircraft after the flight. I found after a couple of days that there was a top-off fueling the next morning before flight, so we added that to the total. The aircraft were always fueled to the maximum because the fuel gauges did not work. The crew's method of determining the fuel remaining at any time was for the flight engineer to record fuel flow and multiple it by the time between readings. I soon found out that not all sergeants do math with the same degree of accuracy! It was also obvious that some engineers were padding the fuel flow so that they always had plenty of fuel which sometimes resulted in shorter missions, and others did not have clue as to how much they had left and landed dangerously short of fuel, considering the fact that Korat had a single runway and the nearest suitable alternate airfield was over a hundred miles away. The other disconcerting thing about the fuel business was that the fuel flow gauges had never been calibrated for accuracy since leaving Lockheed many years before.

All four engines feathered simultaneously over Khe Sanh

I was assigned to an investigation board to look into the incident involving an EC-121 that the crew claimed had experienced simultaneous failure of all four engines while on orbit near Khe Sanh. The aircraft commander was the flying safety officer in the Wing and very experienced in the 121. The crew claimed that suddenly all four engines feathered. Naturally everyone got their chutes on and proceeded to the rear door ready for bail-out. The crew was unable to open the door and had no option but to try to get a couple of engines running to get to Da Nang. This they did and landed without incident. The ground crew could not find anything wrong with the engines or props. But the aircraft could not be flown until an investigation board made a recommendation to Seventh Air Force, in Saigon, and a decision made as to how to proceed.

The majority of the board wanted to go forward with a recommendation that the rear door be wired open, a minimum crew fly the airplane out of Da Nang, and see what happened. I said that was nuts and would not agree to the recommendation. The president of the board said I would have to write a minority report, which I did and got the flight surgeon to sign it with me. When Seventh Air Force got the report, their almost exact response was, "Are you guys crazy? You're not flying that airplane until you find out what happened."

No one could figure out why the door could not be opened during the investigation, but in my discussing this with Colonel Ostendorf recently, it came to light that in their haste to try and get out, the crew had probably forgotten to de-pressurize the aircraft, which would have caused the problem.

Hootch Girl's go-aheads nailed to floor

The hootch I eventually spent the rest of my Bat Cat tour in was inhabited by a bunch of nuts. I roomed with the only other major in the hootch and the other six were great Lt. Col's. We drank a bit, had a lot of laughs and teased the hootch girl. She really was more than a girl, she was actually a grandmother. She laughed a lot, but really didn't understand English too well. She was very graceful and when she arrived in regular street clothes to work she removed her shoes and slipped very gracefully into her go-aheads and never stopped. One of our fun-loving LC's had nailed them to the floor one day and she had quite a start when she was stopped dead in her tracks. The next day my shower clogs were nailed to the ceiling; she thought that was really funny. I never knew who did it.

Where did I leave that Jeep?

The Lt. Col. I relieved as Standardization Board Chief couldn't wait to tell me in confidence that the key to our desk also fit the Operations Officer's Jeep. One day I saw the Ops Officer, pretty well inebriated, park the jeep at the BX and go in. I drove the Jeep off to the warehouse area and parked it. I went back and watched him come out. He couldn't figure our what the hell happened to his Jeep and finally walked away. I don't know how he got it back, but he did.

Lt. Colonel DeWitt Barwick

I first encountered De Barwick when I reported to McClellan AFB, North Highlands, CA. He was an assistant Operations Officer, self-appointed I believe. He was 6' plus and thought that anyone under 6' must have committed a mortal sin to be so short and often said so. His other claim to fame was that he had been flying C121s since the first one came to McClellan. He claimed to never have read the Flight Manual on the airplane. It was obvious it was true because he was quite a loner in his procedures.

He reported to Korat a couple of months after I had become Squadron Standardization Officer. Another Lt. Col., Murray Warden, who had also been at McClellan with us, told him that Clawson asked a hundred questions on the qualifying flight in the Bat Cat aircraft and that he had better read the Manual. Murray told me that he had really been studying because he would not give that SOB Clawson the satisfaction of flunking him. After the pre-flight he said, "Okay ask me your stupid questions".

I said that I didn't intend to ask him any questions since it had been reported to me that he had been studying hard and that's all I wanted. He stormed off, mad as hell. The take-off was spectacular; he pulled the aircraft up to a maximum climb attitude and left METO power on longer than usual. When he had reached his limit and was going to have to push-over, I pulled a simulated engine out. It went that way the whole flight.

One morning about 0300 when it was raining like hell, I knew Barwick was flying with a crew so I got my flight clothes on and rode my bicycle to the flight shack. I told the duty operations Sergeant to put my name on the Flight Orders, which already had about 23 people on it. All the while, Barwick was ranting and raving at me that I was not going with them. He even took this long Flight Order and tore it up. This required the Sergeant to type it all over again. I told Barwick that I could not understand his attitude and I was sure that Colonel Ostendorf, the Wing Commander, would have trouble with it too. He sweetened up and I had no trouble with him until I got after him for letting the pilot land short on the final landing.

Requested Red Cross to check on my Family

My family was notorious for not writing letters and I had not heard from anyone for quite a while, and since they had recently moved I didn't even have a phone number for them. Because of all the anti-war protests we had decided to have an unlisted number. I requested that the Red Cross check on them and see if there was any trouble. About this time, we had one of the two fatal crashes of a Bat Cat aircraft. The family had called McClellan to find out what unit had suffered the accident. Since College Eye crews were still going TDY to Korat, they base information officer quickly assured my family that it was not a McClellan crew, but the other outfit. About this time a deputy sheriff, in uniform, showed up at the house in response to the Red Cross request to check on my family. Even though I had told the family any number of times that if something happened to me, an Air Force officer, accompanied by a chaplain driving and official Air Force vehicle, would notify them, they panicked until the sheriff could explain the purpose of his visit.

"Change Major Brown's ER, nobody is that good"

As Chief of Stan Eval I had special crew-members assigned to check the specialties on the crew. However, they were also assigned to a combat crew. I had a separate combat crew that I flew regular missions with. Through some way, which I can't recall, I was Major Thomas Brown's reporting officer. He was the Stan Eval navigator and a real outstanding officer and navigator. In the combat environment we were in, most every crew-member received very good ratings. I knew Tom was way above the guy who was getting almost perfect reports, so I resolved to give him a real "walk on water" type Officer Effectiveness Report (OER).

The report was superb, and the Squadron Commander endorsed it, concurring with my assessment. Even though the DCO did not sign the report, he reviewed it before it went to the Wing Commander for endorsement. He sent it back to the Squadron Commander with orders to change it, saying, "Nobody is that good." My effectiveness report had already been completed by the Squadron Commander and I was headed home. I had always played the game when told to do something like this, but was fed up with it and refused to change it. The Squadron Commander became livid and said that I was going home, but he had to stay and live with the SOB (the DCO). I made a deal with him, I would have it re-typed and would mark it the same way and then he could downgrade it and that would make the DCO happy. That's what we did and when I went to sign the new report, the old one with the Squadron Commander's endorsement was on the other side of the folder. Naturally, I picked up and took it with me. I went to personnel to see if my report had gone to Hawaii yet. The master sergeant, after hearing my story, said, "No, but it will be." He put into an envelope and he and I walked out to the front of the building and put it in the US Mail. My next stop was the Judge Advocate General's office. The attorneys wanted me to forgo my port call and file charges against the Squadron Commander for attempting to coerce me into changing an official report.

When I rode my bicycle back to the hutch I was met by two or three of these LCs I lived with and they wanted to know what in the hell I'd done. They said the Squadron Commander had called a half a dozen times ordering me to get my ass back to the squadron as fast as I could. When I got to the squadron, I grabbed the executive officer and said I needed a witness and went into the old man's office. He stood me in a brace and read me my rights and then said, "Where the hell is the original report!"

I said I didn't know, and that was truthful, because when I had exited the office after signing the new report, I had given the purloined one to Tom Brown and told him to keep it safe, we may need it. We finally returned the old report, mainly because I was really afraid the Squadron Commander was going to have a stroke or heart attack.

Before leaving, just short of when I was leaving, Colonel Ted Ostendorf had given the new Wing Commander the names of three individuals he wanted no harm to come to. I was one of them. The new Wing Commander had earlier called me and told me this and said he wanted to have a chat with me before I went home. I thought now was the time, called him, set a meeting and discussed the whole matter. He was adamant that I keep my port call, go home and he would take care of Major Brown for me. True to his word, the report was downgraded, DCO was happy, and the Wing Commander dissented and raised the report back to "walk on water".

As I was leaving all the guys in the hootch said they didn't know what they were going to do for fun once I left. I'll bet they found something to do, they were great guys.

FINAL MISSION

"You're 200' below Minimums"-"Shut Up!"

My last Bat Cat mission was started on a Saturday evening and ended on Sunday morning, fairly early. I elected to make a Non-Directional Beacon (NDB) instrument approach even though the weather was clear. I had been studying this approach for a while and felt it would provide a fitting goodbye to all the officers in the wing. The approach had you passing right by the tower, across the runway, heading directly for the Officers' Club. The officer's hootches were all around the O'Club. The approach called for eventual descent to about 500' with a low visibility approach around to the runway. I had a substitute co-pilot and I had not exactly been forthcoming with my intentions, so as I let down I went to about 250—300' above the ground and he's calling out that I was so much below minimums and I kept telling him to shut up. The weather was clear and as we approached overhead of the O'club, I started to bring the throttles forward, with the engineer restraining any rapid movements, and heard that I had emptied the O'club and the hootches. When we parked and I started down the steps from the rear door, the Wing Commander, Colonel Ted Ostendorf, was standing under the steps with a loaded fire hose, and I finished coming down, sopping wet.

> *I made my port call and had a nice ride home on Continental Airlines into Travis AFB and we took some leave and drove to Omaha. I was still in the dark as to what I was going to be doing at the big hall. My new boss had written me a letter assuring me that I knew more abut my new job than I understood yet.*

Chapter IX: Strategic Air Command Headquarters

3902 OPERATIONS SQUADRON
OFFUTT AFB, OMAHA, NEBRASKA
JANUARY 1970—OCTOBER 1973

The assignment to Strategic Air Command (SAC) Headquarters was a surprise to me, even though I had been told by Air Force Personnel in San Antonio that they were reassigning me to SAC. I was sure I was going back to crew duty. I was later told that some field grade officers being assigned to SAC from overseas tours were considered for headquarters assignments first. If not picked up by a directorate their folders then went to numbered Air Force headquarters, and if not chosen there on to a unit. My new boss said that he was the first to see my folder and was impressed.

Because of the classification of the assignment I had no idea what all the clearances were for and no idea of what I was to do in the assignment. After some time and my clearances hadn't come through, my boss expressed some concern. I had filled all the paperwork out before leaving Korat and the clearances should have been in. I told him maybe they were misdirected, since I had a cousin named Clawson, a master sergeant in the SAC Command Post. He left in a hurry and went to see someone and the next day my clearances were available.

Cantwell to Clawson: "What the hell did you do?

Every officer at SAC Headquarters was compelled to join the local civilian organization called AKSARBEN, which is Nebraska spelled backwards. If you didn't join your OER might contain a phrase like "exercises poor judgment". It was futile to resist. I called the civilian office in town and asked two questions and made one observation. They were:

> 1.Who pays for the fancy ball that only a few of the big shots were allowed to attend each year?

2. Requested a real budget to see how the membership dues were spent.
3. Made an observation that my daughter (Maureen) and I attended the Lawrence Welk show in Omaha, sponsored by AKSARBEN, and did not see one black person in the building, either in the audience or working in one of the concessions; requested comment.

That afternoon I received a call at home from the Deputy Chief of Staff—Intelligence (DCS—I) executive officer, who I had been stationed with at Davis Monthan asking me if I had called AKSARBEN today. I said I had. He told me I had a 0800 meeting the next morning scheduled with B/Gen. Johnson in his office. Gen. Johnson was the Deputy Commander for Personnel (DCP) for all of SAC. My boss, Lt. Col. Cantwell, did not know anything about this. I spent an hour with Gen. Johnson. He said he had review my entire personnel folder and found that I was not known as a troublemaker and he said he was also surprised to find that I was not black. He also acted troubled that I thought General Cordes, the Deputy Commander for Intelligence (DCI) and my big boss, would coerce any of his officers to join AKSARBEN. He finally laughed at that too. I had never voiced any objection to paying my dues, so they couldn't figure out what I was up to.

When I returned to my office, Cantwell started yelling at me about "what the hell had I done?" He told me I had a meeting scheduled with General Cordes, the DCI, in 10 minutes, "So get the hell downstairs". Cordes tried to give me hell for creating a ruckus with the fathers of the City of Omaha, but finally gave up on that and told me to keep my nose clean. I still had to explain to Cantwell what I had done. We all had a good laugh about it, but I never received any answers or comments from AKSARBEN.

Near perfect score initial checkout, Convair C-131

It was such a great feeling to be assigned to an aircraft that did not required the services of a flight engineer that I went wild studying for this checkout. The base commander saw fit to write a letter through channels recognizing that it was very unusual to achieve a Highly Qualified status on initial checkout. This really didn't impress the navigators I was working for, though. The letter is reproduced in Figure 19.

"They aren't worth a damn"

The lieutenant colonel I was replacing in the Target Development section was a navigator and so I took a lot or razzing about being a driver. Since I had graduated from navigation school and was rated as a navigator, I wore my navigator wings on my blouse one day. When the colonel saw them he ripped his off his shirt and threw them across the room saying that they weren't worth a damn.

Commander's Call

An Air Force Regulation required a Commander's Call periodically for the purpose of disseminating information and policies that impact on the units performance. Since all SAC officers assigned to the headquarters for duty were technically assigned to the 3902 Operations Squadron, Offutt AFB, we were subject to this requirement. No one I knew at the headquarters even knew where the headquarters for the squadron was on the base. The Commander of a unit is present to allow personnel to ask questions, complain, or make fools of themselves in front of the hierarchy. When first assigned to my job, after waiting for clearances, I saw notices of the Commander's Call to be held in the SAC auditorium, but no one seemed to respond to them. One such announcement encouraged me to go to the auditorium at the appointed hour, and there on a sandwich board at the open door to the auditorium was an agenda and time of the meeting. The lights were on in the auditorium, but I was the only one there. Even the commander, whom no one ever saw, was not there. When I returned and asked my boss why he wasn't at the Commander's Call, and he looked at me like I was some kind of nut. He said nobody ever goes to that, it is just a requirement that those of us at higher headquarters didn't have to comply with. It was tradition. Just more *Alice in Wonderland*.

Bus ride home from Topeka

On my last flight before being excused from flying due to my tour of duty ending within two years, I flew a courier flight in a

Convair that took us to Barksdale AFB, Louisiana, Carswell AFB, Fort Worth, Texas and McConnell AFB, Wichita, Kansas. We changed command of the airplane at Carswell and I was flying as co-pilot in the right seat for the return trip.

We had a very low ceiling on take-off from McConnell, probably right at the legal minimums of 200-foot ceiling and 1/2 mile visibility. At about 300 feet in the air the right engine started acting up and one of the passengers, who were mostly pilots, said we were streaming oil. The engine ran okay otherwise, though, and we elected to keep it running, transferring oil to the engine frequently. We decided to head for Forbes AFB, Topeka, Kansas. The air traffic controller asked when we intended to feather the bad engine, at the same time the pilot pulled the throttles to start descent and the airplane rumbled and shook. While my hand went to feather bottom, I told him, "Right now." The pilot in command had not landed many airplanes with one engine out and one left. He was high and fast, which necessitated some assistance. We got on the ground without incident. The maintenance people determined that the engine had to be changed before flying again so we had to go by surface transportation to reach Offutt AFB.

The base brought out an Air Force bus to return all of us to Omaha. One of the inspectors, a major, was a ground equipment specialist and proceeded to inspect the bus; it flunked and we were another couple of hours waiting for them to fix it. It happened that the people we had picked up at Carswell were a SAC safety team, one of who was the editor or the SAC Safety Magazine *Air Crew*. We received a commendation and our pictures in the next edition of the magazine. We really got razzed about it from our contemporaries.

Vice Admiral Michaelis wants Head in his cabin

Every Air Force general officer in SAC headquarters had elaborate offices with a dressing room and complete toilet and bathing facilities next to them. They were truly impressive. The Director of the Joint Strategic Target Planning Staff, the J-3 for the JCS, was also the Commander-in-Chief Strategic Air Command (CINCSAC). His Deputy Director, a three star admiral had offices (cabin) on the first level underground in SAC Headquarters. During my stay Vice Admiral Michaelis held this position. I got to know him some and one of his objectives while at the JSTPS as to get a toilet (head) facility in his cabin. It was necessary for him to go down the hall and use the communal lavatory during his entire stay. The Air Force was not about to afford him any such luxury.

Michaelis attempts move of JSTPS to Norfolk

We happened to know CINSAC's chief of protocol, who sat right outside the CINC's office. He told us of a conversation between the CINC and the Admiral that involved chewing the Admiral out unmercifully for lobbying in Washington, DC to move the JSTPS to Norfolk, Virginia. Protocol said he had never heard such language, and he had worked in several command posts where that sort of thing went on all the time.

Joe Cantwell's response to JSTPS's threat to get me

Many times wearing a dual hat gave a person heartburn. The directions received from my SAC bosses, many times colonels and generals, conflicted with those from my straight JSTPS bosses. I worked for both of them and it is hard to serve two masters. I was threatened outright one time by my JSTPS boss to support their position at Defense Intelligence Agency or they would get me. I asked Joe Cantwell, my SAC mentor, how to handle it. He said I should re-read my orders sending me to Omaha. He reminded me that I was assigned to the Director of Intelligence, SAC, with additional duty with the JSTPS. He said that as long as I followed my SAC bosses' instructions, any report the JSTPS might add to my Officer Effectiveness Report (OER) that was detrimental to my career would be tossed out.

Don't tell those goddamned civilians anything

Targets List Division full Colonel admonished me to refrain from telling those "god damned civilians any thing at the Defense Intelligence Agency and the CIA.

Major Merl Crabb, Major, US Marines

This character and his wife were the most fun of anyone at SAC

Headquarters. His wife was a wheeler-dealer and pushed Crabb to be the same with very little success. He was our "Mushroom Fairy". He collected wild mushrooms, which we all ate. They had adopted a Korean orphan girl, who was the most independent two-year-old you have ever seen.

A replacement naval officer, a full commander, joined our staff from the Office of Naval Operations. He was a pompous ass, but Merl handled him fine. One day when this jack ass was spouting how his "men" always had a hot cup of coffee on his desk, Merl warned him that about the time he asked one of the Army or Air Force sergeants working in the office for a cup of coffee and he had better be prepared to wear it.

One day after listening to Joe Cantwell rant at me about a message I had written to Air Force Intelligence at the Pentagon, Merl gave Joe a message he needed to have signed off, with multiple choices for most words in the text, cracking Joe up pretty good.

"Where the hell did you guys come from?"

Major Harry Welles was an officer in the targets division I was in and had a different category of targets than I did, but we both were expected at a meeting at the Defense Intelligence Agency (DIA) in Washington one day. Something had delayed us and we thought we would miss the meeting, so we called our contact at DIA and explained our problem. Then we started thinking, we'd somehow heard the Commander-in-Chief, Strategic Air Command (CINSAC) was headed to the Pentagon, and we knew the SAC Protocol Officer, by now Lt. Col. Royal T. Squires from Griffiss AFB and before that Davis Monthan, who sat right outside the CINC's door. I called him and asked if there was a possibility of getting on the CINC's airplane; he said sure, and put us on the manifest. We rushed out to the airplane and flew to Andrews AFB outside Washington. When we arrived there was a helicopter parked almost at the bottom of the stairs of the airplane, we asked the Aide if we could bum a ride to the Pentagon and again, we lucked out. We hit the Pentagon running, caught a cab and arrived at the meeting place ten minutes early. The DIA staff anticipated that we would never make it, and said,

"Where the hell did you guys come from?" We had the meeting and had a good laugh, because it was all luck that we got there at all.

Motormouth trainee—Chicago Center

On a flight to Wurtsmith AFB, Michigan, to pick up a SAC inspection team, we were delayed landing for an hour or so while we waited for the weather to lift to minimums. Finally we landed, picked up the team and started back to Omaha. North-west of Chicago, Minneapolis Center handed us over to Chicago. The first thing I heard was a lot of yelling about where did we come from, they had no radar contact, and on and on. When we got him calmed down by calling back to Minneapolis and asking for them to re-contact Chicago, we finally were recognized. I had never had this happen before, ever, so when we got back to Omaha, I called Omaha Approach Control and discussed our experience the day before. The controller investigated and found that the person we were talking to was a trainee and his instructor told the Omaha controller that the guy was a motormouth and he could not shut him up, but that they had us all the time he was yelling at me.

How to empty red wine on to white tablecloth

We liked to entertain in our home in Papillion, Nebraska, and one Saturday night we invited my boss and the Army Major in our office and their wives to dinner. We had set a very nice table, with white linen tablecloth and crystal and our finest Noritake china. We were serving a prime rib, so we had red wine, which was poured just before we all went to seat ourselves at the table. We all made it but the Army Major. He was about 6'2" and a large guy. He sat down and hit the leg of the table hidden by the tablecloth so hard that it emptied all of the wine glasses on the table. The poor guy was mortified, and no one said a word about what had just happened. We went on with the dinner; still no one said anything. Monday morning our boss, Joe Cantwell, who didn't come up to the Major's shoulder, started in on him about what clumsy ox he was and ruining the Clawsons' tablecloth. It probably would have been better if someone had said something Saturday night, it wouldn't have been so bloody.

Colonel Eugene Freeman, Director of Targets and Roof Fixer

Colonel Eugene Freeman was Director of Targets under the Deputy Chief of Staff—Intelligence. He had a deputy, another full colonel, and a large staff under him. He had also been at SAC Headquarters several times over the years.

One day a Lt. Colonel from another section of the headquarters that I knew asked me if I knew that Colonel Freeman fixed roofs for pay. I was sure that wasn't true but he insisted that Freeman had come to his door in town wearing work clothes and driving an old model station wagon with ladders on the top and various types of roofing material in the car and ask him if he could fix the roof. He would only charge him $10. There was a small bit of damage on the roof and he had him fix it. This was during the business day that ordinarily would have had him in his office at the headquarters.

Soon after that we were at another of our many social outings with people from the base. I was talking to his deputy and ask him if he knew anything about the roof fixing business that Freeman was supposed to be in. He said that it was probably true because when he was at Freeman's house one day he asked what he was saving all the roofing material for. Freeman's answer was that it might come in handy some day.

Lt. Commander Eddie

Eddie was a hapless soul. He had been in charge of a reserve function in New Orleans and against all common sense sent out thousands of SECRET documents in the regular mail to reservists. That was the end of promotions for him.

The AF Master Sergeant in our office would wait until Eddie, who was tall and thin, got his feet on his desk, twisted them around to stay up there and go to sleep. As soon as he was sound asleep, this Sergeant would go to the computer room and dial the classified phone on Eddie's computer terminal. This thing would wake the dead and Eddie would crash and burn trying to get to it.

"You can't send a message like that to Higher Headquarters"

When I first arrived in my new job at SAC, the then Director of Targets told me that my predecessor had neglected to improve on targeting techniques and he wanted me to get off my derrière and do a better job of perfecting the targets I was responsible for than had been done so far. With that I started to travel some, talk to the right people at the Pentagon and other places, and came up with some very advanced thinking about what the other side's intentions might be with their large-scale weapons.

As a result of finding contractor material that could help our effort, Air Force Intelligence found out about it and didn't want me to share any of it with the JSTPS. They contended that this would not be the proper use of the material and I wrote a rather hot message to send to the Pentagon. My boss, Joe Cantwell, blew up and said I could send such a message to higher headquarters. We watered it down and tried to get the Director of Targets to sign off on it and he said the same thing.

Our SAC boss, a Lt. Colonel, and General Cordes, went back a long way and he had been talking to the General about the problem. A meeting was set up to brief the General and as I got to slide two he said, "Don, sounds like Air Force is trying to screw you over." I said, "Yes." He said, send them a message and tell them to go… (physically impossible).

Joe Cantwell, ever cautious with the protocol, made me keep the message watered down and we went back to the Director of Targets. He read it and hit the roof; he said the General had told me to tell them to go… themselves. Joe Cantwell threw the message at me when we were out of the Director's office and said, "Do whatever you want to, I wash my hands of the whole thing."

If You Can't Dazzle Them with Brilliance…

One thing I did a lot of was briefings. Generals, Admirals, Colonels and high-level civilians along with analysts from all the major intelligence agencies in the Government, were interested in surface-to-surface missiles and what we were planning to do with regard to countering them in case of conflict. My wife did not know what I was briefing, but knew I was in front of a lot of people from time to time, so she found Snoopy somewhere and bought it for me. I had view graphs made of it and used it from time to time. Had to watch it, though, when I got to the defense contractor I worked for after retirement because one of my bosses thought it would offend the customer (Figure 20).

"What you're saying is…" No, Sir!

I provided a briefing to the JSTPS Scientific Advisory Group (SAG) regarding some of our findings using the DMAAC and DARPA material. It was pretty obvious that some conclusions could be reached that differed with SAC policy regarding targets. As I briefed the material some of the scientists wanted to jump to the same conclusions I saw, but was forbidden to express. One of the advisors asked me that very question, saying that was what I was saying. I quickly said he had not understood me, but I smiled at him.

"You're going to have to pay back all your salary"

I had been recalled to extended active duty as a National Guard officer, even kept my National Guard suffix to my serial number. One day when we had finished our work early at the Pentagon, Joe Cantwell and I checked with National Guard Bureau in the Pentagon to find that no National Guard Officers are allowed on extended active duty. Joe immediately said I would have to pay back all my pay because I was not legally on active duty and had taken my pay under false pretenses. The National Guard Bureau office at the Pentagon immediately called Wyoming and started the ball rolling to get me discharged from the National Guard and enroll me in the reserves.

"You can pay for your own room"

Another major and myself felt our boss, Joe Schmidt, was having to pay too much for a single room when there were three of us in Washington. We were almost ready to offer to pay part of his room when we saw him exiting his room, with a lady we knew on his arm. We then told him he could pay for his own room.

"Send a message"

Harry Welles, Major, USAF was often accused of peddling his organ all over town. (He sold pianos and musical organs on his off time.) Lt. Col. Norm Bersanti, our SAC boss, didn't like him too much and so seldom allowed him to travel. I'd come out of Bersanti's office with my travel orders signed every time.

Bersanti's remark to him several times was, "Send a message."

"You can't talk to a Senior Officer like that"

Cantwell told me I couldn't talk to a senior officer like I did. A Lt. Col. in the Contingency Section wanted me as Vault Security Officer to open another door to let his visitors in because they did not have proper clearances to get through the door with a security inspector on it. I defended what I had told them and Joe gave up.

"What's this, Sir?"—"A Caulking gun!"

After the first several instances of hijacking commercial airliners, the Air Force thought it would be good to check what the passengers were taking on the Air Force courier airplanes that carried passengers. I was going to the West Coast and was intending to do some work on my fathers house and needed some tools. The person checking my bag was a young airman and he asked me what a particular tool was; I answered that was a caulking gun. He jumped straight in the air at the sound of "gun".

"What! No Purple Heart?"

We had a Marine Lt. Col. working in our office. The office was an open bay so everyone could hear him talking to his Den Mother (personnel) in Washington. He got off the phone somewhat disturbed. The person in Washington had been reviewing the colonel's personnel file and told him everything looked great, he had all the various assignments to give him a look of being a well-rounded officer until he looked at the decorations. He made a big deal out of the lack of a Purple Heart, which shook the colonel up pretty bad. How could he have overlooked such a thing in his career development?

Major Bob Collins, USA, relating Panmunjom experience

As Honor Guard Commander of UN Forces at Panmunjom, Korea, he had the Guard at attention for presentation of what they thought was the equivalent of our Army's Good Conduct Medal. Instead the British Army Sergeant was awarded a medal for 20 years of Undetected Crime.

The dumb bastard started crying—Willie Sonntag

I was standing at the front door of SAC Headquarters waiting for something and all of a sudden my legs were pushed in from the back. I turned and there was Colonel Willie Sonntag. He was headed for the BOQ so he invited me to have a drink with him at the O'Club. It was fun talking to him about the good old days. He said things had changed too much for him. He related that he was chewing an officer out one day for something he probably hadn't done and he said he couldn't believe it, but the dumb bastard started crying.

He also related how one day he was on the phone with the spot Lieutenant Colonel at Griffiss who was chief of Stan Eval, the same one who wrote the letters to the Air Inspectors, and he hung up on Willie in the middle of the chewing out he was getting. Willie said he knew where he was in another building and he ran like hell and caught and really chewed him out.

Staff Visit to Little Rock Missile Base

I made several staff visits to operating missile sites to become more familiar with procedures so I could understand what I was evaluating for Target Development of other people's missiles. Also it allowed me to learn more about missile vulnerabilities. Colonel Don LaMoine was Wing Commander. At the stand up briefing the morning after my arrival Colonel LaMoine introduced me with, "Major Clawson has more clearances than any of you can imagine. If he asks you a question and you know the answer, he is cleared to hear it." Colonel LaMoine was in the back seat of my B-47 at Davis Monthan that lost the shimmy dampener during a 30-bottle ATO assisted take-off and aborted the mission, probably saving our lives.

Penetration by Security Personnel into SAC Command Post

While I was at SAC Headquarters, the security people made one successful covert penetration all the way into the SAC Command Post. Heads really rolled, and many of the Elite Guard were back guarding B-52s at Minot AFB. How they could have done this was really a mystery to me. Security at SAC was taken very seriously most of the time.

"Clear the halls!"

One of the first things I was briefed on when I was cleared into the underground at SAC Headquarters was the requirement the Elite Guard (Air Police) had to reach any point in the building within an extremely short time. This meant that two or more of these big brutes (most over 6') with clubs and guns strapped on them would run at full tilt down the halls, calling out as they went, "Clear the halls!" It was strange to see a general with his back up against the wall as tight as he could get it to get out of the way.

Trip to St, Louis with Navy Captains

The JSTPS had many submarine officers assigned to SAC Headquarters. It seemed that none of them were over 5'6" tall. As a group they had an inordinate fear of flying. We took several of them to St. Louis one time to visit the Defense Mapping Agency. One of the other pilots in our section and I put in for a Convair to make the trip and the captains were uneasy about the whole thing, but went along. We arrived at the St. Louis Airport just as the sun was coming up and it sat right on the end of the runway making it very difficult to make the approach. The other pilot was a fast thinker so he simply held a map up in front of my face and I continued an ILS approach and when I reached the end of the runway, he pulled it back and said, "*Now,*" and I pulled back on the wheel and landed. The Navy Captains saw all this and weren't too impressed. They really didn't want to ride home with us, but had no choice.

Who the hell is paying for all of this?

Because the targets I was responsible were the hot issue of the day (Ballistic Missiles) many agencies were tasked to provide answers regarding the deployment and use of the foreign missiles. We established a good rapport with the analysts at CIA, NSA, DIA and the Defense Mapping Agency Aeronautical Center (DMAAC) in Saint Louis, Missouri. The work that SAC was able to accomplish regarding the deployment and vulnerabilities of foreign ballistic force was valuable to the other agencies so many meetings were set up for these agencies to visit SAC Headquarters and I was the point man for the project. The only thing my bosses had to say about all the people being there was, "Who is paying for all this?" I told them I didn't know, but we weren't.

Since I was a reserve officer I was required to retire after 20 years of active duty. This date was October 30, 1973. I was offered a reasonably well-paying job with the defense contractor I had been working with through their contracting officer, so I moved to Morgan Hill, California and worked for another 16 years.

As nutty as the Air Force had been, the private side of the military-industrial complex was sheer lunacy. But that's another story.

Epilog

Throughout this book I have given my thoughts about the quality of personnel, peers, subordinates and superiors. In general, all of the officers I served with met a minimum level of competency. Some were very good, most were at a level of accomplishing just what was required to keep going. Some were outstanding, though not many in the middle range of ranks—captain through lieutenant colonel. The greatest problem with competency came from the system of choosing commanders and staff officers by date of rank. The only command position that was not filled in this manner that I'm personally familiar with was the SAC Wing Commander. The date of rank method in selecting the Vice Wing Commander was certainly used.

The Strategic Air Command had trouble attaining combat ready status with the B-52 force before deactivation of B-47 units because the only crews a Wing would nominate for BUF training were the ones that had pulled the last bonehead trick before the quota had to be filled. (See Davis Monthan anecdote "B-47 Crew—Mayday".) Eventually SAC Headquarters directed which crew would be selected and finally had to freeze the composition of that crew to prevent substitutions. You had to get up early in the morning to think faster than a Wing Commander, trying to get that star.

Given the Air Force attitude toward the Soviet Union and the possibility of pre-emptive strikes as proposed by Major General Orville Anderson, Commandant of the Air War College, the complete reliance on crew integrity is very troubling in retrospect. At the time the crews were completely aware of what could have been done by a renegade crew-member in the way of executing the entire SAC Airborne Alert Force. It is true that once General Anderson announced his proposal of "preventive war", he was retired almost immediately; politically he had committed suicide and he had to be renounced. What does not ring true, though, is if his views were so bad politically why was he brought back for at least five years to lecture the very officers who would be the Air Force leaders in the future, and allowed to propose the very thing he was fired for?

Since training messages in the clear on HF frequencies simulating a strike order were sent three times an hour for many, many years in relatively the same format, it would be interesting to know if the Soviets knew the exact format for an execution message, training being green and execution being red. If they did, this would give them many hours, in some cases, to bring their air defense system to a high state of readiness.

This attitude prevailed among the highest authorities in the Defense Department. The Joint Chiefs were clamoring for strikes against Cuba. General Taylor wanted strikes not "later than Monday Morning, the 29th". Secretary McNamara went ballistic upon hearing of an engagement with Soviet defense forces saying, "This means war with the Soviet Union." Even after the Soviets issued orders to cease construction of the missile sites and to start dismantling the weapons, which had been described by President Kennedy as "offensive", General Curtis LeMay forcefully argued that the United States "go in and make a strike anyway".

The fact that as far as is it known, no incident of any crew-member doing anything other that his duty is a great credit to the crews and the commanders who selected these individuals for such duty. The fact that nothing happened is not because adequate safeguards were in place; it was a fortunate outcome of inadequate planning at the very highest level.

We small people were constantly told that we did not understand the big picture, but when placed in a position of observing, or advising people making "big picture" decisions we have all found that the decision makers were in many cases lacking in knowledge. A good case in point is the original Strategic Defense Initiative proposal for the terminal phase. This involved placing 100 radars, equally spaced around the United States, to be based on active military bases and deployed to the assigned position by railroad. After three years of this architecture, it was pointed out that there were no railroads in most of the deployment areas. This surprised the Army Defense Command and the whole idea was dropped from the next iteration of the architecture without ever explaining why it was not such a good idea. Someone in authority had not questioned this "bright idea".

I doubt that the National Command Authority (NCA) had any idea that the primary crew-members on each airborne alert B-52 had such a capability and were aware of the awesome burden they carried. On the other hand it could be that some of these people understood only too well what the crews could have done and maybe expected them to initiate a strike.

The citizens of the old Soviet Union had no idea of how much they owe to the integrity of the crew-members of all the B-52s. They were flying around the clock and around the world with nuclear weapons that would have annihilated them if a rogue crew-member had executed the force.

After many years of crew duty and staff work at SAC Headquarters, certain characteristics of the thinking that went into the composition of our forces to fight communism are apparent. The very first thing that is apparent to me is that if a counter to a threat is not possible, the threat does not exist. Example: The TU-16 Badger Bomber of the Soviet Air Force, roughly equivalent to the B-47, was not considered a threat to the CONUS because it was not capable of making a round trip bombing raid and landing back in the Soviet Union. The B-47 targets in the Soviet Union sometimes required landing within 20 minutes of bombs away or bail-out as soon as we were clear of the target area itself. B-47s attacking Leningrad were expected to land at Helsinki International Airport. Reason for the non-threat assessment, the Air Defense system of the United States was not capable of intercepting and destroying even a small portion of such an invading force.

A second non-threat assessment was the vulnerability of SAC B-52 bases in the CONUS. The B-52 in most cases was based at single runway complexes which had all of the alert aircraft lined up neatly on a pad with a single access taxiway to the single runway. The security of the runway and taxiways was imperative to the successful launch of the alert aircraft. Any action on the part of people within mortar distance or grenade launchers or high power rifle could stop the flow of aircraft and negate the threat of the B-52 against the Soviet Union. When this was brought up and a study suggested, it was immediately shut down and no conversation was allowed about the threat. Years later I was privy to many high-cost classified studies regarding this subject. Again; no counter available, no threat.

There is no evidence that Soviet Bombers ever flew with nuclear weapons on board or even loaded them aboard aircraft on ground alert, reflecting a lack of trust by the communist commanders in the air crews.

With so many people writing books about the Cuban Missile Crisis it is inconceivable that so little mention has ever been made regarding the B-52s flying airborne alert with nuclear weapons ready to be dropped merely by arming them and dropping them where the crew decided.

The Soviets were well aware of how many B-52s were airborne simply by monitoring high frequency radio. Each B-52 was required to make an "operation normal" report back to their numbered Air Force Headquarters every hour.

The training messages for the execution message were broadcast three times every hour, twenty-four hours a day for more than 20 years. The format of the message was standard and used color coding to immediately inform the crews what kind of message was being transmitted. It would be very unlikely that the Soviets did not know the color code for the go-code. Once this message was transmitted there was no recall and all SAC Strategic Communications facilities were required to re-broadcast the message until they were put off the air. If the Soviets knew the color coding, this would provide many hours of advance knowledge of a strike.

Addendum

Glossary Of Acronyms, etc.

JCS	Joint Chiefs of Staff
SAC	Strategic Air Command, a specified command under the Joint Chiefs of Staff.
JSTPS	Joint Strategic Target Planning Staff (J3 of JCS)
DNIF	Duty Not Involving Flying (*not* "drunk not interested in flying")
EWO	Emergency War Order
OLT	On-the-Line Trainee (personnel waiting for aircrew training)
KP	Kitchen Police
MP	Military Policeman
Piball	Pilot Balloon sent aloft to measure certain parameters, mostly wind speed and direction.
BX	Base Exchange
WAC	Women Army Corps
AWOL	Absent without official leave
BUF	Big Ugly Fellow (B-52)
CD	Chrome Dome (Airborne Alert-B-52s): unclassified name for the Airborne Alert flown by B-52s with war reserve ammunition and chaff, decoys, large yield nuclear weapons, and some units were equipped with Hound Dog air-to-ground missiles.
ANG	Air National Guard
JAG	Judge Advocate General
Gooney	

bird	C-47 Transport Aircraft
OER	Officer Effectiveness Report
TDY	Temporary Duty (at another station)
Broken arrow	An event involving compromising nuclear weapons safety or security.
MCS	Management Control System: a system of grading everything SAC wings accomplished to determine where problems were. It also was used to select SAC general officers.
Gissy	Informal name assigned to the authentication material worn around the necks of the three primary crew-members on the B-52.
Feet wet	Termed used to describe and airborne vehicle leaving the shoreline and being over water.
TSS	Unknown, 1945 unit term
Spot rank	Select crew-member, SAC bomber force. Wing Commander designated certain crews in the wing as "select" based mainly on navigation and bombing skills of the navigator. The aircraft commander and co-pilot then rode on his coat-tails and all three were given one higher rank. It was temporary, but time spent as a spot promotee counted as time in grade when they were eventually promoted by the promotion board. Other commands had a hard time accepting these spots.
MITO	Minimum interval take-off. Used to put the greatest number of bombers in the air in shortest period of time. The norm was 15 seconds between applying take-off power. Most crews shortened this to 8-10 seconds.
VFR	Visual Flight Rules. See and be seen

IFR	Instrument Flight Rules. Had to file a clearance and have contact with air traffic control.
MARSA	Military assumes responsibility for separation of aircraft.
NCA	National Command Authority. Primarily thought of as the President. There is a devolution of command that has changed some over the years.
Hootch	A building used for almost anything. Mostly housing.
NOTAM	Notice to airman. Announces closures of ground and radio facilities Also any unusual procedures affecting flight.
SOP	Standard Operating Procedures
IP	Instructor Pilot. Can also be used for the Initial Point in a bomb run.

Ratings And Awards

MAJOR LYLE DON CLAWSON
UNITED STATES AIR FORCE, RETIRED

Airplane pilot
16 January 1954

Navigator
13 July 1957

Senior pilot
23 January 1961

Command pilot
16 January 1969

Distinguished flying cross
16 August 1969
For
Extraordinary achievement
while participating in
aerial flight

The meritorious service medal
For
Outstanding service
4 February 1970 to 14 April 1973

Air medal
With
Four oak leaf clusters
1967 to 1969
For
Meritorious achievement

While participating in
Aerial flight

Air force commendation medal
With one oak leaf cluster
For
Military merit

Combat Readiness Medal
Air Force

Good conduct medal
(USAAF)
1 July 1944 to 28 October 1945

American Campaign Medal

World War II Victory Medal
1 July 1944 to 28 October 1945

National Defence Service Medal
With one bronze star

US Vietnam service medal
With 5 bronze stars

Republic of Vietnam
Commendation medal

List Of Aircraft Flown By Clawson

1.	Culver Dart	Parks Air College—1943
2.	Travelaire	Parks Air College—1946
3.	Stearman	Parks Air College—1946 & 1947
4.	Piper Cub	San Fernando, Lone Pine, California; Bainbridge, Ga
5.	T-6 Texan	Bainbridge, Ga and Selma, Alabama
6.	T-28	Lubbock, and San Angelo, Texas
7.	B-25	Lubbock, San Angelo, Texas; Montgomery, Ala.
8.	T-33	Selma, Ala.
9.	B-47	McConnell AFB, Little Rock AFB, Davis Monthan AFB, Arizona
10.	B-52	Griffiss AFB, Rome, NY; Roswell Castle AFB, California
11.	C and EC 121	Cheyenne, WY, ANG; Otis AFB, MA, Tainan City, Taiwan; Korat, Thailand; McClellan AFB
12.	Convair	Omaha, NB
13.	Cessna 172	Merced, CA
14.	Piper Cherokee	San Martin, CA
15.	DC 6/7	United Air Lines, Denver, CO
16.	B-727	United Air Lines, Denver, CO
17.	C-47	Goodfellow AFB, Texas

18. Caravelle   UAL—Trip from
                                 Chicago to Boston

Total pilot time for all of the above aircraft is in excess of
8,000 hours. Total combat time as pilot was about 1,190
hours.

Letters

L. Don Clawson
e-mail: dclawson@jps.net

December 22, 2001

Mr. Robert S. McNamara
700 New Hampshire Ave Nw,
Washington, DC 20037-2406

Dear Sir:

Because you were the Secretary of Defense during the Cuban Missile Crisis I am writing in the hope you will reflect on what you were aware of during that period with respect to the SAC B-52 Airborne Alert missions. In a cursory manner I would like to review what the crews were aware of and roughly what the missions consisted of in the way of armament.

In October, 1962 I was a regular Air Force officer assigned to the Strategic Air Command in the 4039th Strategic Wing at Griffiss AFB, Rome, New York. My duty assignment was as an aircraft commander on the B-52G aircraft. During 1961-62 I flew 15 Chrome Dome missions which carried two G-77 Hound Dog missiles with nuclear warheads and four nuclear weapons in the forward bomb bay. The rear bomb bay contained four GAM-72 Quail (decoys). War reserve chaff and ammunition for the defensive side of the mission completed the Airborne Alert configuration. We usually carried one extra co-pilot to allow some rest for each of the pilots.

One mission was to fly what we called the Thule Monitor and the other was into the Mediterranean to Tripoli and back across Spain and on home. We accomplished two large aerial refuelings over Spain (approximately 126,000 lbs. each) on each mission.

The above weapons were in no way inhibited and were

available for the crew to drop, armed, at any time. The National Command Authority requirement before proceeding to the target area was that we receive a message in the proper format and properly authenticated. We had checklists with the message format pre-printed, and we just filled in the blanks when the message was received over High Frequency radio. The authentication tables hung around each of the three primary crew-members, (pilot, co-pilot and radar navigator) neck.

My inquiry consists of two questions:

1. Were you aware that the crews had the physical capability of dropping the weapons, armed, at any time without any action on the part of the NCA? In other words no electronic interlock or any other inhibitor in connection with dropping the weapons.

2. Did you as Secretary of Defense realize that any one of the primary crew-members on the airborne alert B-52s could construct a valid, authenticated message? This message could have been broadcast using the high frequency radio, on the aircraft, and execute the entire B-52 airborne alert force with no possibility of a recall of the airborne aircraft. Was this possibility ever discussed?

Having retired from active duty in 1973 after 122 missions out of Korat, Thailand in EC-121s supporting the Igloo White and College Eye Projects I have had time to reflect on how much the Air Force and the Government relied on the integrity of the B-52 crews. It is surprising how little has been said about their work. I would very much appreciate a response to my questions.

Yours truly
L. Don Clawson

L. Don Clawson
e-mail: dclawson@jps.net

December 27, 2001

Major General Andrey G. Marshankin
Defense Attaché
Embassy of the Russian Federation
2552 Belmont Road NW
Washington, D. C. 20008

Dear Sir:

During the Cuban Missile Crisis of October 1962 Prime Minister Nikita Krushchev of the Soviet Union was aware of the US Air Force's Strategic Air Command's (SAC) B-52 Airborne Alert (Chrome Dome) missions. He stated for attribution that 20% of the SAC B-52 force was on Airborne Alert during the latter part of October 1962.

Each B-52 crew made an operations normal report on high frequency (HF) radio to their higher headquarters every hour. This was done partly to keep the commanders apprised of their current status and partly to allow the Soviet "listeners" to report the number of aircraft in the air. In addition three times every hour a message was transmitted on HF radio by SAC headquarters or other command entities to all airborne SAC aircraft which had a color code identifier. This was usually a training message and sometimes conveyed other information. This message was transmitted thousands of times over almost thirty years.

In October 1962 I was a regular US Air Force officer assigned to the Strategic Air Command in the 4039th Strategic Wing at Griffiss AFB, Rome, New York. My duty assignment was as an aircraft commander on the B-52G aircraft. During 1961-62 I flew 15 Chrome Dome (Airborne Alert) missions. I am retired now and am trying to write an account of my service life. This was a very scary time in the history of mankind and I would like to put my part of it into the proper prospective.

My question is this:

Did the Soviet "listeners" know what the color code or format of a US command to the B-52s to strike their targets would be? Would it have enabled them to flag such a message for the Soviet High Command? Such knowledge would have provided time to launch retaliatory missiles and provide warning to the Soviet Air Defense System. Was the above part of the "listeners" standard operating procedure?

Any insight you can provide concerning how the B-52 airborne alert during the Cuban Missile Crisis in October 1962 was perceived by the Soviet Defense establishment would be of great help in further understanding how close we all were to a terrible disaster.

Yours truly,
Don Clawson